THE ART OF POLITICAL MANIPULATION

Keech

P9-CDH-736

WILLIAM H. RIKER

THE ART OF POLITICAL MANIPULATION

Yale University Press
New Haven and London

Designed by Nancy Ovedovitz and set in Times Roman type by Huron Valley. Printed in the United States of America by Vail-Ballou Press, Binghamton, NY.

Library of Congress Cataloging-in-Publication Data
Riker, William H.
    The art of political manipulation.
    1. Political leadership.   2. Political planning.
3. Games of strategy (Mathematics)   I. Title.
JA74.R53   1986   303.3'4   85-22448
ISBN 0-300-03591-8
ISBN 0-300-03592-6 (pbk.)

The paper in this book meets the guidelines for permanence and durability of the Committee on Production Guidelines for Book Longevity of the Council on Library Resources.

10 9 8 7 6 5 4 3 2 1

To Jessica, Marguerite, and Catherine

CONTENTS

PREFACE

Heresthetic is a word I have coined to refer to a political strategy. Its root is a Greek word for choosing and electing. While it is related to rhetoric, the art of verbal persuasion, still heresthetic differs from rhetoric because there is a lot more than eloquence and elegance involved in heresthetic. It is true that people win politically because they have induced other people to join them in alliances and coalitions. But the winners induce by more than rhetorical attraction. Typically they win because they have set up the situation in such a way that other people will want to join them—or will feel forced by circumstances to join them—even without any persuasion at all. And this is what heresthetic is about: structuring the world so you can win.

Heresthetic is an art, not a science. There is no set of scientific laws that can be more or less mechanically applied to generate successful strategies. Instead, the novice heresthetician must learn by practice how to go about managing and manipulating and maneuvering to get the decisions he or she wants. Practice is, however, difficult to engage in, especially since one must win often enough to become a political leader before one has much opportunity to practice. There is one partial substitute for practice, however, and that is the vicarious experience of instruction. Unfortunately, instruction is also hard to come by, because the literature of heresthetic is fugitive, consisting mostly of occasional comments and stories in books about politics and politicians. Consequently, there is a real need for more copious illustrative instruction. I hope this book will help to fill it.

Had heresthetic been properly recognized as an art by some of its practitioners, it would have been, from classical times onward, one of the liberal arts, which are the arts that free men use to control their surroundings. There are several liberal arts of language, and heresthetic would have been one of them because the heresthetician uses language to manipulate other people. He talks to them, asking them questions and telling them facts; he utters arguments, giving reasons for believing his arguments are true; and he describes social nature, importing to his description the exact twist that leads others to respond to nature as he wishes.

The traditional liberal arts of language are logic, rhetoric, and grammar and it is easy to see how heresthetic parallels them. Logic is concerned with the truth-value of sentences. Grammar is concerned with the communications-value of sentences. Rhetoric is concerned with the persuasion-value of sentences. And heresthetic is concerned with the strategy-value of sentences. In each case, the art involves the use of language to accomplish some purpose: to arrive at truth, to communicate, to persuade, and to manipulate.

The liberal arts of language were originally developed in order to catalogue and inventory practical knowledge about their uses. But in recent times philosophers and scientists have recognized that cataloguing and inventorying are not enough. To develop practical subjects, it is necessary, as it turns out, to systematize them. And this requires general theory about each of the subject matters. Once theoretical knowledge exists, it is then possible to investigate the subjects without waiting for more or less accidental and random developments in the practice of the arts. Finally, once theory itself is elaborated, it offers new insights into practice. For example, the art of medicine—that is, the actual and practical cure of patients—is now always taught within the context of the preclinical theoretical sciences, which are only remotely concerned with the practice of medicine itself. So it is with the liberal arts of language. In recent times, they have been embedded in more complex intellectual constructs:

> *logic,* in the theory of knowledge and the philosophy of science;
> *grammar,* in linguistics;
> *rhetoric,* in psychology and semantics.

Heresthetic, however, is the product of a reverse history. Its theory was developed first and was followed with the recognition that, along with the theory, there was a practical art of great significance for the life of free men. The theory is social choice theory (or, as it is sometimes called, decision theory), which is a specialized branch of economic theory and political theory. Social choice theory consists of descriptions and analyses of the way that the preferences of individual members of a group are amalgamated into a decision for the group as a whole: how committee members' values are aggregated into an adopted motion; how the selection of officials reflects—or does not reflect—constituents' preferences; how auction markets and decentralized trading amalgamate the tastes of participants; etc., etc.

Naturally, in all these processes, strategic manipulation plays a fundamental part. Indeed, one part of social choice theory is the theory of games of strategy. So as social choice theory developed, theorists also began to compile concrete instances of applications of the theory. This compilation is, of course, exactly like the compilation of examples of rhetorical events or of logical and grammatical rules. And thus, from these compilations, was born heresthetic, or the art of manipulation, as a practical supplement to a new, but swiftly developing, theory.

In turn, in this book I am offering a part of this compilation to the public, so that men of affairs may be instructed in this newly rationalized liberal art. The book thus consists of twelve stories, followed by a conclusion that contains a bit of the theory on which my interpretations rest.

ACKNOWLEDGMENTS

Most of the stories in this book were workd out as classroom examples. Consequently, my initial and greatest debt is to my students. In response to my expositions of theory, however neat and surprising, they have asked, perhaps reasonably, "What on earth does all this have to do with the real world?" These stories are part of my answer, and I appreciate the skeptical queries of those students who thereby provided inspiration, criticism, and, above all, an audience.

I am grateful as well to the officers of those foundations whose support gave me the occasional leisure to write these stories: The Joseph Chamberlin Wilson and Marie Curran Wilson professorships at the University of Rochester, the Guggenheim Foundation, and the Political Economy program at Washington University where I served in 1983–84 as a visiting research professor.

My most immediate debt is to those friends who have discussed these stories with me and helped me improve them: James Alt, Steven Brams, Bruce Bueno de Mesquita, William Chaney, the late Maurice Cunningham, Arthur Denzau, Richard Fenno, Evelyn Fink, Michael Levine, Richard Niemi, Charles Plott, Bingham Powell, Kenneth Shepsle, and Richard Smith. They have instructed me and encouraged me and I thank them very much.

William H. Riker

University of Rochester
September 22, 1985

1 LINCOLN AT FREEPORT

For a person who expects to lose on some decision, the fundamental heresthetical device is to divide the majority with a new alternative, one that he prefers to the alternative previously expected to win. If successful, this maneuver produces a new majority coalition composed of the old minority and the portion of the old majority that likes the new alternative better. Of course, it takes artistic creativity of the highest order to invent precisely the right kind of new alternative. The products of heresthetical genius are ephemeral compared to the work of, say, a great inventor, a great painter, or a great mathematician, though the heresthetical creations usually have more immediate impact on the world. Still the level of genius and creativity is roughly the same for the heresthetician as for these other innovators, and ought, I believe, to be admired and respected for exactly the same reasons.

So, as an appropriate illustration of both heresthetic and genius, I take my first example from the work of Abraham Lincoln, the greatest of American politicians and a man equally skilled as a heresthetician and a rhetorician. This example, which was recognized as a work of genius soon after its use, was a trap, much in the spirit of a dilemma, so cleverly constructed that no matter how the opponent responded the response itself would give Lincoln or his friends a future victory.

In the summer of 1858 Lincoln and Stephen Douglas, the incumbent Democratic senator, were campaigning for the election of candidates for the Illinois legislature who were pledged to vote for them for the United States Senate. The campaign took the form, in part, of a series of debates in Illinois cities, and in the debate at Freeport, Lincoln asked Douglas the question that ensnared him. The question was: "Can the people of a United States Territory, in any lawful way, against the wish of any citizen of the United States, exclude slavery from its limits prior to the formation of a state constitution?" To modern readers this question probably seems legalistic in sense and turgid in expression, and probably some are astonished by my description of it as a work of genius. However, it was not just the words themselves, but the setting, that honed this question stiletto-sharp.

Throughout the whole period from 1800 to 1864 the coalition, variously revised, of Federalists, National Republicans, Whigs, and finally Republicans probably elected only one president with a majority of the popular vote.* Conversely, the coalition of Jeffersonian Republican-Democrats, revised into Jacksonian Democrats, elected at least ten by a majority. And from 1801 to 1869, Federalist-Whig-Republicans occupied the White House for only about 16 years, while Democrats occupied it for 52 years. Clearly the latter party was by far the more successful, doubtless because throughout the entire time it stood on a platform of agrarian expansionism, while the Federalist to Republican coalition stood on a platform of commercial expansionism. Given the fact that the great majority of the people worked in agriculture, it is not strange that the Democrats won most of the time. It is odd indeed that the Federalist-Whig-Republicans ever won at all.

Naturally, they repeatedly tried realigning themselves on some new organizing principle, which explains the sequence of new names, Federalist to National Republican to Whig to Republican. Along the way some adherents tried out other kinds of parties—Anti-Masonic, Know-Nothing (anti-immigrant), and Liberty or Free Soil (antislavery); and on occasion even Whigs deserted their central theme of commercial expansion. In 1840, for example, when they for once won a majority, they presented, on a platform of agrarian expansion, the aged Indian-killer, William Henry Harrison, the hero of Tippecanoe (1810), a rather faint carbon copy of Andrew Jackson, the

---

*He was William Henry Harrison. I do not count Lincoln in 1864 because he was elected on a Union ticket—union with War Democrats like his vice-president, Andrew Jackson—only by a majority in a truncated nation.

greatest Indian-killer of them all, and even a far less gory copy of Richard Johnson (Van Buren's vice-president), who with his own knife in his own hand killed Tecumseh.

Of all these alternative organizing principles, the most attractive and, increasingly, the most effective was some version of antislavery. The constitutional compromise in 1787 impliedly made slavery a matter of local law, and it was therefore not admitted to national discussion for over thirty years. But in 1819, even though he personally had been a party to the Compromise of 1787, Rufus King, the last Federalist candidate for president in 1816, tried to revive the fortunes of his defunct party by leading the great national burst of outrage over the motion to admit Missouri into the Union as a slave state. Jefferson, old and brooding at Monticello, described the agitation as a "fire-bell in the night," recognizing it for what it truly was: the instrument by which his coalition would eventually be undone. But not right away. Federalists became Whigs and attracted many Southerners, which made the slavery issue a less attractive tactic. Whigs used it only when they were out of office. But use it they did. John Quincy Adams, who, as president, had shown no particular sympathy for the condition of blacks, became the trumpet of righteousness denouncing slavery in the District of Columbia, clearly a national subject, and organizing Northern Whigs around free soil. By 1846, Northern Democrats were so terrified by the prospect of defeat on this issue that they embraced the antislavery position themselves (in, for example, the support of the Wilmot Proviso and the Van Buren candidacy in 1848). When the Whigs realized that they could do better by sloughing off their Southern adherents and attracting these radical Northern Democrats, they regrouped as the Republican party. This was something new, Federalist and Whig commercial expansionism tied to antislavery which, in its free-soil form of prohibition of slavery in territories and thus in all future states, was a kind of agrarian expansionism too. Finally, the core of the Federalist-Whig-Republican coalition had found an issue on which it could win. From 1868 to 1928 it elected nine presidents by a majority and held the White House 48 out of 64 years, while the Democrats elected no president by a majority and held the White House

only 16 of those 64 years, thereby almost exactly reversing the
party fortunes in the previous era.

Democrats knew, of course, what damage the slavery issue
could do to them. President Polk, writing in 1847, attributed
the raising of the question, probably correctly, to Whig opportunism and prophesied the effect with remarkable accuracy:

> The slavery question is assuming a fearful and most important
> aspect. The movement [for the Wilmot Proviso] . . . if persevered
> in, will be attended with terrible consequences to the country, and
> cannot fail to destroy the Democratic party, if it does not ulti-
> mately destroy the Union itself. . . . Of course, Federalists [Polk's
> pejorative name for Whigs] are delighted to see such a question
> agitated by Northern Democrats because it divides and distracts the
> Democratic party and increases their [that is, Whig's] prospects of
> coming to power. Such an agitation is not only unwise but wicked.

The Democratic response to the slavery issue was, therefore,
to paper it over, to push it back into the localities so that it
could not be agitated nationally. In the 1850s the main Democratic device for this response was the Kansas-Nebraska Act of
1854, which was mainly the handiwork of Stephen A. Douglas.
It provided that territorial legislatures, not Congress, should
decide on whether or not to permit slavery in territories. It did
not work. Civil war in "bleeding Kansas" was the result. And
then the Southern Democratic majority on the Supreme Court
took the occasion of the Dred Scott case (1857) to rule that a
slave was not a citizen and had no standing in federal court to
sue even though resident in a free territory, and that, by impli-
cation, territorial laws against slavery conflicted with the Constitution. This decision profoundly shocked most Northerners,
and—quite blindly, so it appeared—blocked Douglas's strategy. But radical Southerners were delighted and the decision
encouraged them to raise their reservation price in intraparti-
san bargaining from a simple demand for toleration of their
"peculiar institution" to an overweening demand for the right
to expand the institution throughout the territories.

This, then, was the setting for Lincoln's question. It came
out of the long Whig search for a winning issue; out of the
ultimate realization that the slavery issue would irreparably

split the Democratic party, and had indeed split it at the formation of the Republican party; and out of the opportunity offered by the intensity of feeling, North and South, on the Dred Scott decision to exploit even more adroitly the division in the Democracy.

Lincoln's question generated a personal and political dilemma for Douglas. He was running for reelection as senator in 1858, but as the leading Northern Democrat, he also hoped and expected to be the Democratic candidate for president in 1860. These two elections were in two different constituencies, Illinois and the nation as a whole, in which the divisions of opinion were quite different. And it was this difference that Lincoln exploited.

If Douglas answered yes (that territorial legislatures could exclude slavery), then he would please Northern Democrats for the Illinois election. This would continue his policy of pushing the slavery issue back to the territories and, for Illinois Democratic voters, it would seem adequately free-soil in tone. On the other hand, for the radical Southerners, now wholly intransigent after the Dred Scott decision, yes would seem a betrayal of the Southern cause of the expansion of slave territory and a split in the traditional intersectional Democratic alliance. So a yes answer improved his chances in Illinois in 1858 but severely hurt his chances in the nation in 1860.

On the other hand, if Douglas answered no, then he would appear to capitulate entirely to the Southern wing of the party and alienate free-soil Illinois Democrats. Thus he would hurt his chances in Illinois in 1858 but help his chances for 1860.

Since he had to answer either yes or no, he was certain to hurt himself in one of the two elections.

Douglas answered yes and was reelected to the Senate. But in the nominating convention in 1860 he was nominated only after Southerners withdrew in order to nominate a third candidate for themselves. Lincoln won the Republican nomination, in no small part because of the heresthetical ability displayed in the campaign of 1858, and was elected president by a plurality.

His question at Freeport should be interpreted, I think, as the capstone of the Republican strategy of splitting the Democratic majority. As between the traditional platforms of agrarian expansionism (Democratic and majority) and commercial expansionism (Whig and minority), the Republican combination of commerce and free-soil attracted the Northern Whigs (a large majority of that party) and a substantial proportion of Northern Democrats, so that Republicans had, first, a plurality and, by 1868, a big majority in the nation. I think there is no more elegant example of the heresthetical device of splitting the majority, and it displays Lincoln the politician at his grandest.

An interesting incidental question is whether or not Lincoln in 1858 foresaw his own role in 1860. The debates were certainly one of the very first public campaigns for the Senate and, for that reason alone, attracted national attention; and Lincoln himself took care to get the debates published in Ohio in 1859, all of which suggests that Lincoln may have had some plans for his own future. There seems to be no question, however, that he saw the Freeport question as a way to destroy Douglas and split the Democratic party in 1860. His campaign advisors opposed his asking the question, and it is hard to find any motive for Lincoln to ask it other than a self-sacrificing attempt to undo the Democrats. In his historical novel *The Crisis,* Winston Churchill—the American novelist, not the British statesman—romanticized Lincoln's heresthetic at Freeport by attributing to him the following parable, where the pear is the senatorship and Sue Bell is the presidency:

> "Boys," said he, "did you ever hear the story of farmer Bell, down in Egypt? I'll tell it to you, boys, and then perhaps you'll know why I'll ask Judge Douglas that question. Farmer Bell had the prize Bartlett pear tree, and the prettiest gal in that section. And he thought about the same of each of 'em. All the boys were after Sue Bell. But there was only one who had any chance of getting her, and his name was Jim Rickets. Jim was the handsomest man in that section. He's been hung since. But Jim had a good deal out of life,—all the appetites, and some of the gratifications. He liked Sue, and he liked a luscious Bartlett. And he intended to have both. And it just so happened that that prize pear tree had a whopper on that year, and old man Bell couldn't talk of anything else.

"Now there was an ugly galoot whose name isn't worth mentioning. He knew he wasn't in any way fit for Sue and he liked pears about as well as Jim Rickets. Well one night here comes Jim along the road, whistling, to court Susan, and there was the ugly galoot a-yearning on the bank under the pear tree. Jim was all fixed up, and he says to the galoot, 'Let's have a throw.' Now the galoot knew old Bell was looking over the fence. So he says, 'All right,' and he gives Jim the first shot. Jim fetched down the big pear, got his teeth in it and strolled off to the house, kind of pitiful of the galoot for a half-witted ass. When he got to the door, there was the old man. 'What are you here for?' says he. 'Why,' says Rickets, in his off-handed way, for he always had great confidence, 'to fetch Sue.'

"The old man used to wear brass toes to keep his boots from wearing out," said Mr. Lincoln, dreamily.

"You see," continued Mr. Lincoln, "you see the galoot knew that Jim Rickets wasn't to be trusted with Susan Bell."

AN ENDNOTE ON THE RELATION OF HERESTHETIC TO RHETORIC

The dilemma is a classic rhetorical device intended to show the logical weakness of an opponent's intellectual position. It persuades by revealing the opponent's weakness and implying thereby the speaker's strength. A standard example that goes back to early fifth-century Greek culture—actually to the colonial culture of Syracuse in Sicily—is the double dilemma of Korax (the "crow") and Tisias. Korax, a rhetor and sophist, was the teacher of Tisias (and also of Gorgias, who became a great teacher of rhetoric in Athens and the subject of Plato's dialogue of that name, through which he made *sophist* a pejorative word for all time). Tisias had agreed to pay tuition to Korax out of the fee from the first case he won. But he did not practice and so did not pay. Korax sued and Tisias defended himself with this dilemma: "If I win, I need not pay by reason of the judgment of the court. If I lose, I need not pay because the terms of the contract will not have been fulfilled. Since I must either win or lose, I need not pay." Korax responded: "If I win, you must pay by reason of the judgment of the court. If I lose you must pay because the terms of the contract will then be fulfilled. Since I must either win or lose, you must pay."

The judge dismissed the case (so Tisias won), but the judge called him a "bad egg from a bad crow." So in a sense neither dilemma was rhetorically successful because each canceled the other out. Doubtless Korax did, however, achieve enormous word-of-mouth advertising, as indicated by this repetition of the story twenty-four centuries later.

In these rhetorical dilemmas the purpose is to show that the opponent's case is weak. But in the heresthetical dilemma Lincoln posed to Douglas the purpose was to force Douglas to put himself in an undesirable position for winning some future election. Clearly the goal of the rhetorical dilemma is to persuade, while that of the heresthetical dilemma is to structure the decision-making situation to the speaker's advantage and the respondent's disadvantage.

This contrast is in general true of all parallels between rhetoric and heresthetic. It might be thought that rhetoricians would have collected examples of heresthetic as well as rhetoric. Indeed, one of the reasons I have derived the word *heresthetic* from a Greek root is that Greeks should have, but did not, identify the heresthetic art. The reason they did not, I believe, is that rhetoric and heresthetic are fundamentally different. Having chosen to concentrate on rhetoric, they never got around to the study of heresthetic, even though they unconsciously practiced it in their popular assemblies.

Sources: The exact form of Lincoln's question and Douglas's response is most easily available in A. Lincoln, *The Illinois Political Campaign of 1858: A Facsimile of the Printer's Copies of His Debates with Stephen Arnold Douglas as Edited and Prepared for the Press by Abraham Lincoln* (Washington, D.C.: Library of Congress, 1958). An account of the development of the slavery issue is contained in chapter 9 of my book, *Liberalism against Populism: A Confrontation between the Theory of Democracy and the Theory of Social Choice* (San Francisco: W. H. Freeman, 1982). The quotation from President Polk is from James K. Polk, *Diary,* ed. Milo M. Quaife, 4 vols., (Chicago: McClurg, 1910), January 4, 1847, vol. 2, p. 305. The story of Farmer Bell, Jim Rickets, and the ugly galoot is from Winston Churchill, *The Crisis* (New York: The Macmillan Co., 1901), part 2, chapter 3. The story of Korax and Tisias is most easily available in George Kennedy, *The Art of Persuasion in Greece* (Princeton, N.J.: Princeton University Press, 1963), pp. 59ff.

2 CHAUNCEY DEPEW AND THE SEVENTEENTH AMENDMENT

Most people conventionally assume that social decisions are made by straightforwardly amalgamating the opinions of some relevant people—in an oligarchy, those of oligarchs; in a democracy, those of citizen-voters. Of course, if amalgamation really were that simple, then most heresthetical devices (like splitting the majority) would not work. Actually, of course, amalgamation is not at all simple, as is easy to see in the paradox of voting, a neat puzzle that reveals a bit of the astonishing complexity of amalgamation. To illustrate the paradox, assume three people (1, 2, 3) who choose among three alternatives (*a, b, c*) by majority rule in pairwise contests. Assume also that those people order their preferences transitively, which means that:

if *a* is preferred to *b* and *b* to *c* then *a* is preferred to *c*—or, in short form, *abc*.

Finally, let the people order their preferences thus

1. *abc*
2. *bca*
3. *cab*

Then, *a* beats *b* (by the votes of 1 and 3), *b* beats *c* (by the votes of 1 and 2), and *c* beats *a* (by the votes of 2 and 3). So the amalgamated preferences are circular (intransitive): *abca*, even though each individual's preferences are transitive. Rational man and irrational society.

When tastes are circular (and if there are three or more alternatives and two or more voters, then almost always tastes are at least potentially circular), then the outcome depends as much on the procedure of amalgamation as on the tastes of participants. Hence, it is always possible to manipulate the outcome by manipulating the agenda. For example, assume in the foregoing illustration that people use the amendment procedure (as in legislatures) so that, say, a is put against b and the winner against c. With that agenda, c wins. But if a is put against c initially, then b wins. Or if b is put against c initially, a wins. Thus, each alternative can win under some agenda. Naturally members of legislatures expend considerable energy trying to get control of the agenda.

The obvious way to control the agenda is to be the presiding officer or a member of the committee on the agenda (for example, the Rules Committee in the House of Representatives). A large proportion of the dispute between political parties consists of efforts to get and keep these positions. But it is also possible for ordinary members to control the agenda by exploitation of the rules of the body.

Heresthetic concerns both kinds of control, by leaders and by ordinary members, and I will offer some examples of each. But control by ordinary members is the most spectacular, so I begin with the amazing story of Chauncey DePew, who, simply by offering a cleverly formed amendment, delayed for about ten years the adoption of the Seventeenth Amendment to the U.S. Constitution (on the direct election of senators).

Before he was senator from New York, DePew spent over thirty years working for the Vanderbilts. Initially, he was their man in politics, a lobbyist and lawyer, but eventually he became president of the New York Central Railroad and thus their chief public relations man. After that he served two terms (1899–1911) in the Senate. In the era of trust-building and trust-busting, he was, of course, a controversial figure. For those who admired trust-builders he was a great man—and deservedly so, because he was one of the old Commodore's chief agents in his greatest accomplishment, namely, combining enough small railroads to run, as early as 1873, a scheduled train from New York to Chicago in twenty-four hours! To trust-busters, on the other hand, DePew epitomized all that was supposedly wrong in the politics of commercial expansionism. Whatever the ultimate judgment on his whole career, however, it must be granted, I think, that he was an enormously talented heresthetician, which is a useful skill for both P.R. men and senators.

The framers of the Constitution provided that, since the Senate was intended to represent the states, state legislatures would elect senators. But, as it soon turned out, the Senate never did represent state governments as intended, mainly because the framers failed to provide a way by which state legislatures could discipline senators if they voted contrary to legislatures' instructions. Hence, from the very beginning, there was no real justification for indirect election because the Constitutional system would not be significantly changed if election were made direct. Whether elections were direct or indirect was thus no more than a matter of taste. By the latter part of the nineteenth century popular tastes were opposed to indirect election because corruption in senatorial elections had become a national scandal. (In the mining states of the West, the price of a legislator's vote for a senator was said to be $2,000, occasionally rising, as tight contests approached decision, to $5,000.) In the 1890s therefore, direct or popular election of senators became a conventional progressive proposal, and resolutions to amend the Constitution to provide for it regularly passed the House of Representatives—and never got out of committee in the Senate.

Senators prized their political freedom. It was easy and dignified to run for the Senate—mainly because one did not have to run at all. Unlike the Illinois campaign of 1858 with its candidates' debates, almost all nineteenth-century senatorial campaigns did not even begin until after state legislators were elected, and then the campaigns consisted almost entirely of soliciting the votes of one or two hundred state legislators. Naturally, senators were not eager to subject themselves to the discomforts of a public campaign, certainly not in response to jealous and malicious resolutions from the House.* But the senators had no real defense since indirect election had never served its original purpose of providing representation for state governments.

Gradually even senators themselves joined the agitation for popular election. Beginning in the 1890s the system of primary elections spread rapidly through the states, in the South because the so-called white primary was a device to disfranchise blacks and in the North because the primary was a "progressive" reform. Hence many senators came to be elected directly, for all practical purposes, after arduous primary campaigns; and they became ardent advocates of direct election. Most northeastern states resisted primaries, but still, indirect election was doomed. Chauncey DePew, from a northeastern state, did, however, prolong the indirect system for another ten years.

In 1902 a proposed Constitutional amendment passed the House in a form substantially equivalent to the first clause of the present Seventeenth Amendment, which reads, in relevant part:

> The Senate of the United States shall be composed of two Senators from each state, elected by the people thereof, for six years; and each Senator shall have one vote. The electors in each state shall have the qualifications requisite for electors of the most numerous branch of the state legislature.

For the first time such an amendment was actually considered by a Senate committee. Chauncey DePew then introduced his amendment, which the committee accepted and reported. The report was never brought to a vote, however, because De-

---

*Chauncey DePew, writing twenty years later and after the Seventeenth Amendment had deprived senators of their freedom from campaigning, still thought the six-year term made the Senate a better place than the House: "My twelve years in the Senate were among the happiest in my life. The Senate has long enjoyed the reputation of being the best club in the world, but it is more than that. . . . there is an independence in a term of six years, which is of enormous value to the legislative work of the Senator. The member of the House, who is compelled to go before his district every two years, must spend most of his time looking after re-election" (*My Memories of Eighty Years* [New York: Charles Scribners' Sons, 1922], p. 175). Perhaps the Senate was such an exclusive club at the turn of the century because the dollar price of membership was so high.

Pew's amendment effectively killed the Constitutional amendment. As an addition to the Constitutional amendment, the
DePew amendment read:

> The qualifications of citizens entitled to vote for United States
> Senators and Representatives in Congress shall be uniform in all
> states, and Congress shall have the power to enforce this article by
> appropriate legislation and to provide for the registration of citi-
> zens entitled to vote, the conduct of such elections, and the certifi-
> cation of the result.

Today this sentence seems innocuous enough, but in the political context of 1902 it was a killer. It was, in the language of
the era, a "force bill." The only elections that might turn out
differently if federally regulated were, of course, in the South,
where regulation would reenfranchise blacks. But the threat to
Democrats was even more pointed. The words *to enforce* and
to provide for . . . the conduct of elections recalled the era of
Reconstruction, then only twenty-five years before. DePew in
effect proposed to give Constitutional authority for the revival
of Reconstruction, for putting the army in the South to super-
vise elections, and for guaranteeing the election of some black
(and even white) Republicans. What the DePew amendment
said to Southern senators, and indeed to Democratic senators
generally, was: "You can have your direct election if you
really want it, but the price is the reimposition of Reconstruction and honest elections and hence a lot more Republicans."
No Southern senator was willing to pay a price that high.

It is conceivable—unlikely but conceivable—that the proposed Constitutional amendment could, even in 1902, have
been passed by a two-thirds majority composed of Southern
and Northern Democrats and midwestern and western Republicans. But surely, without the Southern Democrats the Constitutional amendment would fail. That was the first thing the
DePew amendment did: It alienated the Southern Democrats
from the Constitutional amendment.

Why, you may ask, would it not be possible for this putative
two-thirds majority to remove the DePew amendment so as to
render the Constitutional amendment palatable to the white

South? But this, too, was impossible and that was the sneaky power of the DePew amendment.

If there was any issue upon which the Republican party was united in that era it was the desirability of fair treatment for blacks. No Republican would wish or dare to vote for a motion unfriendly to blacks—and a motion to delete the DePew amendment would, of course, be regarded as unfriendly. Even those western Republicans who favored the Constitutional amendment and were fully aware that they were being manipulated by DePew would fear to vote against the amendment. Thus the Republican majority in the Senate was a clear majority for the DePew amendment. Hence there was, possibly, a cycle: The DePew amendment beat the Constitutional amendment, which—perhaps—beat the status quo, which in turn beat the DePew amendment. So the constitutional amendment was doomed.

It may seem to some readers that this is a rather fanciful tale to tell about a motion that never even got to the floor of the Senate. But we can be pretty sure it is just about true because the Constitutional amendment did get to the floor nine years later, along with a reverse version of the DePew amendment. In February 1911, the Constitutional amendment was reported with what might be called a "protective clause" for Southern racism: "The times, places, and manner of holding elections for Senators shall be prescribed by the legislatures thereof [i.e., of the States]." But the opponents of direct election could not be foreclosed so easily. Senator Sutherland of Utah introduced an amendment to delete the protective clause—the reverse of the DePew amendment but with the equivalent parliamentary effect. There were thus three alternatives before the Senate:

(a) The resolution to amend the Constitution as amended by the Sutherland amendment (i.e., the resolution without the protective clause);

(b) the resolution to amend the Constitution as originally reported (i.e., with the protective clause);

(c) no action.

At the time of the roll calls the Senate had 88 members present, so a simple majority was 45 and a two-thirds majority was 57. The vote on the Sutherland amendment pitted *a* against *b*. The Sutherland amendment won, 50 to 36, so the survivor was *a*. The second vote, on the now amended resolution, pitted *a* against *c*. The resolution failed by 54 yea to 34 nay—57 votes yea were Constitutionally required to pass the resolution—so *c* was the social choice. To estimate the relation of *b* to *c* (i.e., to estimate the chance that the *un*amended resolution might have passed if it had ever come to vote), we can assume that all 54 (or at least 53 of them) who voted yea on the amended resolution—*a* over *c*—also favored the unamended resolution, *b* over *c*.* We also know that eight Southern Democrats, led by John Sharp Williams of Mississippi, had insisted on the protective clause and, when it was deleted, voted against the Constitutional amendment, that is, for *c* over *a*. Clearly they favored *b* over *c*, making a total of at least 61 or well over the two-thirds required. Thus *b* would have been the social choice had the original resolution been voted on directly. This gives us a clear cycle:

a beats *b* (as voted on)
b beats *c* (as estimated)
c beats *a* (as voted on)

So the Sutherland amendment had exactly the effect I imputed to the DePew amendment.

There is a footnote to this story. The cycle occurred in a

---

*Those who voted nay on the Sutherland amendment and yea on the Constitutional amendment as amended must have ordered *bac*. They included 20 Northern and Border Democrats and eight western Republicans. Those who voted yea on both roll calls might have had either *abc* or *acb*. They were 25 Republicans and one Southern Democrat, who seems to have been confused. These 25 Republicans were exactly those who were being manipulated by the maneuver. They favored the Constitutional amendment, but they were constrained, by their identification as Republicans, to vote to attach the Sutherland amendment. Hence they must have had the preference order *abc* and the order *acb* must have been held by no one (or possibly by the lone Southern Democrat). Thus it seems reasonable to say that either 53 or 54 persons who voted yea on the amended Constitutional amendment favored *b* over *c*.

lame duck session. A few months later Democrats, now with an absolute majority, could prevent the DePew-Sutherland maneuver. Since over half the Republicans were also in favor of direct election, it was then easy to pass the Seventeenth Amendment, even without a protective clause.* But the amendment had been delayed for about ten years because DePew was able to use the ordinary member's power to offer amendments in such a way as to exploit divisions of opinion in the Senate.

The complicated moral of this story is that, while in the long run a widely held opinion is likely to be crystallized into a social decision, the crystallization can often be delayed, probably sometimes indefinitely, by a clever heresthetician.

Sources: Detail on the occasion for the Seventeenth Amendment is set forth in William H. Riker, "The Senate and American Federalism," *American Political Science Review* 49 (June 1955): 452–67. I have told the story of the DePew amendment twice before, once in "Arrow's Theorem and Some Examples of the Paradox of Voting," in John Claunch, ed., *Mathematical Applications in Political Science I* (Dallas: The Arnold Foundation, Southern Methodist University Press, 1965), pp. 41–60, and the second time in *Liberalism against Populism: A Confrontation between the Theory of Democracy and the Theory of Social Choice* (San Francisco: W. H. Freeman, 1982), pp. 192–95.

---

*That is, the majority in favor of the amendment was now so large it was no longer necessary to bribe the eight Southerners.

3 **THE FLYING CLUB**

As I pointed out in the beginning of the previous chapter, one of the main advantages of being the leader of a legislative body, a committee, and the like is that leaders have considerable control over the agenda, sometimes even enough control to determine which motions, bills, amendments, and so on are approved. Both the politicians' folklore and the academic literature on legislatures are replete with tales of presiding officers who recognize only the movers of motions they want to hear and, even more tyrannically, of agenda committees that refuse to propose an agenda until the author of a bill agrees to write it in the way the members of the agenda committee want it written.

I am, on the whole, inclined to believe some of these tales, if only because there are so many of them. The chance that at least one is true seems pretty high. Still, it is always possible that they are all false because, for the most part, these tale-spinners are better at gossip than at handling necessary conditions and contrary-to-fact conditionals. To make the anecdotes believable, one must make credible sentences of the form, "If the Rules Committee had granted the rule (i.e., agenda), then the bill would have passed." It is not easy, however, to accumulate evidence of what might have been.

One pair of social scientists has, however, done exactly that by showing how, in situations of equivalent distributions of preferences, they could design several agendas that would produce victories for different alternatives. In effect, they pointed the bat to right field and hit the ball there, pointed the bat to left field and hit the ball there, and so on—not once, but several times. Hence they have gone beyond mere anecdotes and have offered fairly good evidence that leaders' manipulation of agendas *can* determine outcomes. If so, then, in the natural world outside the laboratory, manipulation probably sometimes *does* determine them. At least their evidence convinces me and I think it will convince you.

It all started when Michael Levine, a professor of law, remarked to Charles Plott, a professor of economics, "Charley, I'm the chairman of an agenda committee of my flying club. We're going to decide on a new fleet. They made me chairman because I'm the only lawyer in the club. But you know a lot more about voting than I do. What's a fair way to do this?"

Plott, who had indeed made a notable mathematical discovery about voting, replied, "Well, Mike, a lot of voting schemes are fair. You ought not to care about equity as much as whether or not some fair scheme will get the fleet you want. Most people think that voting tells you the 'preferences of the group.' But, you know, Mike, groups don't prefer anything. They aren't human beings. Just because we talk about the 'will of the people' doesn't mean the 'will of the people' exists. The choice of a group is cerainly not independent of the process by which it was chosen. So there just isn't any *true* preference of the group. There are various possible outcomes which the different procedures will allow the group to reach. And all these outcomes are in some sense acceptable and fair. But some are more acceptable to one person, and others are more acceptable to another. There's no reason why the club shouldn't choose one you like. Let's see if we can arrange things that way."

After much thought about this novel morality, Levine agreed and the two of them set about planning the agenda.

The flying club, a nonprofit organization, owned and maintained a fleet of airplanes to rent to members. In 1973, when the event occurred, the club had about 65 members (who paid $1,800 to join for capital, $30 per month dues for general maintenance, and rent of about $25 per hour for maintenance of the plane rented) and a fleet of six single-engine planes (three five-year-old Beechcraft E-33As, one three-year-old Beechcraft V-35, one three-year old Beechcraft F-33A, and a new Cessna 210). On the whole the members preferred roomy aircraft capable of fairly high speeds (e.g., 185 mph cruising speed), which tend to be top-of-the-line models; and they were dissatisfied with the current fleet because it was not uniform (a safety consideration since the Beechcraft V-35 and, particularly, the Cessna 210 had different operating characteristics from the others), because the older planes were shabby, because they wanted different and better avionics equipment, and because planes were not always available when members wanted them.

The range of possibilities for the new fleet was limited by the members' clear-cut preference for Beechcraft (presumably more prestigious than other makes) and Cessnas (which were distributed by the larger club of which this club was a subunit), by their preference for eliminating the one V tail aircraft, and by their resources (the equivalent of $100,000 capital and up to $500,000 credit). This meant that the fleet would consist of the four-seated Beechcraft E-33A and F-33A (which was an updated version of E-33A) and possibly six-seated planes, either Beechcraft A-36 or Cessna 210, in all six or seven planes. The four varieties of airplanes differed mainly in capacity and operating cost, as follows:

Manufacturer and Model	Abbreviation Used	Number of Seats	Estimated Rental per Hour
Beechcraft A36	A	6	$31.50
Beechcraft F33A	F	4	$30.00
Beechcraft E33A (refurbished)	E	4	$24.00
Cessna 210	C	6	$27.00

From earlier discussions it appeared that most members preferred Beechcraft, but members of the governing board seemed to want Cessnas, probably because of their Cessna dealership. A few highly influential members wanted Beechcraft A-36s, then the most luxurious and expensive single-engine Beechcraft. On the other hand, many members seemed concerned about expenses. They certainly expected to refurbish the three old E-33As, but they probably didn't want to buy additional E-33As to refurbish.

Levine's main interest was to include in the fleet some six-seated aircraft which could be used for family trips. Of these he preferred the cheaper Cessna 210 to the more expensive Beechcraft A-36. Indeed, if the 210 were included, he would have liked two; if the A-36, only one. In general, he was neutral about buying new F33As or additional E33As to refurbish. So his preference order was:

1. (5E, 2C) or (3E, 2F, 2C)
2. (5E, 1C) or (3E, 2F, 1C)
3. (6E, 1A) or (3E, 3F, 1A)
4. (5E, 2A) or (3E, 2F, 2A)
5. and lower (all E and F)

Levine and Plott believed this differed somewhat from the mainstream of the club, who might prefer an entire fleet of Es and Fs and, if a secondary fleet were accepted, would prefer As to Cs. Hence their problem, as they saw it, was to devise an agenda that would produce a decision for a fleet of mostly Es and Fs with one or two Cs, against a possible majority for a fleet of Es, Fs, and possibly As.

Had Levine desired something radically different (say, all Cs), then their problem would have been insoluble, for he would have been a minority of one. Since, however, his taste differed only marginally from the mainstream, it was feasible to attempt to satisfy him. So they planned an agenda accordingly. Summarized from two pages of typescript and translated from the jargon of aeronautics, it consisted of the following questions to be decided sequentially:

1. What type of aircraft should be the primary fleet? (To be decided by a Borda count.)*
2. How many planes do we want?
3. Do we want a mixed fleet?
4. What type of aircraft should be in our secondary fleet?
5. How elaborately should we equip the aircraft?

---

*In a Borda count over, say, four alternatives, the voter gives three points to his first choice, two to his second, one to his third, and none to his fourth. For each alternative, the points from all the voters are summed and the winner is the alternative with the largest number of points.

The first question was posed as a Borda count, not because they had any doubt of the outcome (namely a preference for Es and Fs), but in order "to put at ease those members who feared being 'stuck' with an expensive fleet [i.e., foisted on them by the influential members who wanted As] and make them agreeable to a seven-plane fleet," which would be more likely to include Cs than would a six-plane one.

The second question was, they thought, the crucial one. Since they believed that a plurality wanted a fleet of six four-seat planes, it was important to pose the question in such a way that this plurality be isolated. They hoped to produce a majority coalition for seven planes consisting of: those who wanted seven four-seaters; those who wanted a mixed fleet (including six-seaters, either As or Cs) and who, hopefully, would recognize that they stood a better chance with a seven-plane fleet than a six-plane one.

The third question was intended to pit all who wanted any kind of six-seat plane (As or Cs) against those who wanted only Es and Fs. Thus Plott and Levine were attempting to use the supporters of As to reach the point at which Cs could beat As. As it turned out their agenda was incomplete, and it was natural and necessary in the course of the meeting, since the mixed-fleet question was answered affirmatively, to insert an additional question, call it 3a: "Should the secondary fleet be one or two planes?"

The fourth agenda question was intended, assuming 2 and 3 were answered favorably, to pit those who favored Cs against those who favored As. Given the expectation that a seven-plane fleet would be adopted, those who were concerned about the expense of seven planes and were otherwise neutral about Cs and As might be expected to vote for Cs.

The question on equipment was saved to the end. Plott and Levine wanted to avoid the possibility that members might initially decide on expensive equipment and then as a result be reluctant to purchase a seven-plane fleet. So they delayed decision on avionics until after the size of the fleet had been determined.

The result of that agenda was impressive. The club tied on

fleets of (3E, 2F, 2C) and of (3E, 2F, 2A), but since the governing board clearly preferred Cs to As, in effect the club chose Levine's first preference. To resolve administrative difficulties after the meeting, a questionnaire was sent to members asking them to rank a number of the alternatives. From this, Plott and Levine were able to reconstruct the preference orders of all those who were at the meeting. Using the data thus constructed, they concluded that, if all the main possibilities for fleets had been put against each other in a round-robin, a fleet of (3E, 3F, A) would have come in first, Levine's preference (3E, 2F, 2C) would have come in second, and the outcome (3E, 2F, 2A), tied with Levine's, would have come in fifth.

Their achievement is all the more impressive because it was carried through in the face of difficulties. For one thing, the votes were taken at precisely the same hour that the famous tennis match between Billie Jean King and Bobby Riggs was being televised. Hence, only the most concerned and presumably the hardest to manipulate members were present. For another thing, the chairman, an ardent supporter of As, attempted several times to rearrange the agenda to favor his preference. At the very beginning before the agenda was introduced, he attempted to put the question "Do we want an all Bonanza [i.e., Beechcraft] fleet?" which, if adopted, would have precluded Cs. Similarly, after the Borda count on the composition of the primary fleet but before question 2 (on its size), he attempted to ask, "Do we want As or Cs as a secondary fleet?" which seemed to Plott and Levine a way to get As chosen before the cost considerations of a seven-plane fleet might preclude them. Finally, after the fleet size (question 2) was decided but before the vote on the size of the secondary fleet (question 3a), he attempted to put the question, "Do we want at least one A?" By coming before the decision on size, this question might well have resulted in a fleet of (3E, 3F, A). According to the calculation of Plott and Levine during the meeting (confirmed afterward by analysis of the data from the post-meeting questionnaire), every one of the chairman's questions would have been answered affirmatively (as he

TABLE 1

Subject of ballot	Actual Vote		Vote Calculated from Questionnaire	
	Six	Seven	Six	Seven
Six or seven Planes?	6	14	6	16
A mixed fleet?	unanimous yea	unanimous yea		
Number of planes in	one	two	one	two
secondary fleet?	unavailable	13	9	12
Cs or As?	C	A	C	A
	10	10	11	9

wished), thus entirely precluding the Cs that were actually selected. To counteract the chairman, the agenda committee stuck rigidly to its agenda, declared his questions out of order, and were sustained by the club on the procedural points.

The actual course of the balloting is shown in table 1. Also shown is the outcome derived by inference from the post-meeting questionnaire. Comparison of the two indicates that the questionnaire reveals tastes very similar to the actual voting. This fact supports, in my opinion, Plott's and Levine's conviction that (3E, 3F, A) would have beaten the winner (3E, 2F, 2C) in a head-to-head contest.

Naturally Plott and Levine were proud of their accomplishment. But they had niggling doubts. Perhaps, they fretted, they had just been lucky, not skillful. Perhaps the particular set of members present would have chosen (3E, 3F, 2C) with nearly any agenda. Tantalized by the uncertainty, they decided to reproduce the whole episode in a series of experiments. Thereby they convinced me that they truly could force the selection of outcomes they predicted ahead of time.

First they abstracted the agenda problem. Suppose, they said, a club is planning a dinner that might be formal or informal in dress and French or Mexican in cuisine. One agenda for decision might be a decision on dress first and cuisine second, thus:

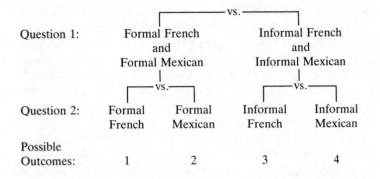

Or the agenda might be reversed, cuisine first and dress second, but the same four outcomes would still be possible. Or, less naturally, the agenda might first place (Formal French, Informal Mexican) against (Informal French, Formal Mexican) and then, for the winning pair, place its two components against each other, again leading to the same four possible outcomes. Thus there are three distinct possible agendas and, if leaders really can control outcomes, they should be able to predict the winning outcome for each agenda and then, by choice of the agenda, bring about an outcome selected ahead of time.

To run their experiment, say, four times, they had to have four groups of voters—different people each time, lest the experience with one agenda contaminate performance with another. But to operate different agendas in equivalent situations, the people in each group had to have exactly the same set of preferences as the people in other groups. To create such an arrangement, Plott and Levine posited a set of five alternatives which, after some false starts, they made totally abstract—the letters A, B, C, D, and E—so that voters would have no previous association with them. They then assigned preferences over these alternatives by promising to pay a particular voter a different amount for the success of each alternative. Thus, in each group, the person in the first position might be promised $6.00 if A was chosen, $7.00 if B, $5.00 if C, $8.00 if D, and $.50 if E; the person in the second position might be promised \$8.00 for A, \$7.50 for B, \$7.00 for C, \$6.00 for D, and \$.25 for E, and so on. These promises thus induced preferences over the five alternatives, however abstract they might be because, manifestly, the first person in each group would surely prefer D to B to A to C to E. Thus, even though each group consisted of different persons, still each group would contain exactly the same set of individual preference orders, as induced by the promised payments.

The one thing that could not be made identical in each group was the way a particular human chooser might go about choosing. Suppose at some step in the agenda the group is supposed to decide between (B, C, E) and (A, D). Suppose some person's (actually, number sixteen's) ordering is C, A, D, B, E because he gets \$7.50 if C wins, \$7.00 for A, \$6.50 for D, \$5.00 for B, and \$.25 for E. Thus he might choose between the sets (B, C, E) and (A, D)

- by a "sincere" strategy, that is by choosing the set with the most desired alternative, here (B, C, E);
- by an "avoid-the-worst" strategy, that is, by choosing the set *not* containing the least liked alternative, here (A, D);
- by an "average value" strategy, that is, by choosing the set with the highest average value, here (A, D), which has an average value of \$6.75, against an average for the alternatives in (B, C, E) of \$4.25;
- by a "sophisticated" strategy, that is, by choosing at step *s* according to the outcome anticipated by the group decision at step *s* plus one;
- by some other unidentified strategy.

Since they had no way of knowing what strategies the voters would use, they calculated from data from pilot experiments the expected frequency with which voters might use the first three strategies. (They omitted strategies they did not know about and the sophisticated strategy because it was unlikely to appear in an experiment of the form used.) Assuming that people with identical tastes choose among these three strategies with the same probabilities, they then could assume also that they had a roughly equivalent set of people in each experiment.

Incidentally, in creating their group of 21 preference orders, they made things harder for themselves by giving one alternative a clear majority over each of the others in a *pairwise* vote. Exactly,

- alternative A beat everything else;
- alternative B beat C, C beat D, and D beat B, a cycle;
- alternative E lost to everything else.

To carry out the experiment they also needed a particular agenda with predicted outcomes. With five alternatives there are at least 120 possible agendas. Not all these are useful, however, because some involve close outcomes at each step, thus rendering prediction difficult. To select agendas, Plott and Levine defined the strength of an agenda (or of an agenda item) as the expectation that the given agenda (or item) would produce a particular winning alternative (or a winning set of alternatives). Using the calculation of strength, they then selected four agendas such that a specific alternative had a strength of one, that is, was almost certain to be chosen. In the first agenda, C was supposed to win; in the second, D; in the third, B; and in the fourth, A.

For each experiment they then chose four groups of 21 students each (recruited by newspaper advertisements in the California Institute of Technology, the University of California at Los Angeles, and the University of Southern California). They also selected several students to serve as presiding officers. The students were told that they were to participate in an experiment about decision making in a meeting lasting about an hour, with no overtly political discussion. They were promised an opportunity, not a certainty, of making somewhat more than the going rate for student labor. They were assured that the experimenters were interested in logical and technical problems of decision making, not psychological or personal variables, and that they would not suffer harm or embarrassment. (This elaborate disclaimer was necessary because students had by 1973 become wary of experiments, having so often been hoodwinked, cheated, embarrassed, and emotionally victimized in thousands of experiments conducted by psychologists.)

Plott and Levine then trained the presiding officer (whom they paid $4.00 per hour) in the conduct of the experiment, being careful not to inform him of the subject of inquiry. (The purpose of this arrangement was to prevent the experimenters from communicating their interest in the outcome to the presiding officer or the voters. Indeed, the whole experiment was "double blind," because only the research assistant, Steven Matthews, knew which alternative was predicted to win. Apparently these precautions were effective. Afterward the chairman of the second, third, and fourth experiments, a Cal Tech senior, confessed, "I never thought of the agenda as the point of the experiments.")

The students for a particular experiment assembled in a classroom at noon and were asked to read the instructions placed at the seat. Each instruction sheet informed the student of the amount of money he/she would be paid for each alternative. No student was allowed to know the amounts promised to others. The instructions also explained how the meeting would be conducted. The experimenter, himself uninformed about which agenda was being tested, outlined the procedure and introduced the chairman and the research assistant, who was identified as the recording secretary and who in fact confined himself silently to his record-keeping duties. The chairman then instructed the students in detail about the procedure and gave them a test to be sure they understood what they were being asked to do.

Once these preliminaries were over, the chairman opened the first item for discussion. Naturally the students were a bit hesitant at first—what can one say to compare (A, C) with (B, D, E)? But, with real differences in potential income, discussion became reasonably widespread. The chairman kept order, ruling out of order questions or comments revealing actual payoffs for alternatives, but allowing such remarks as "A is better for me than B." He also was supposed to prohibit changes in the agenda, although once he improperly allowed a straw vote, an act which Plott and Levine believed significantly changed the agenda and outcome. After "enough" discussion,

FIGURE 1

Agenda—Experiment 1

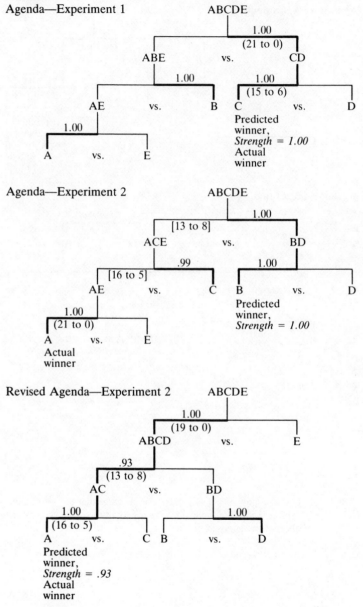

Agenda—Experiment 2

Revised Agenda—Experiment 2

Agenda—Experiment 3

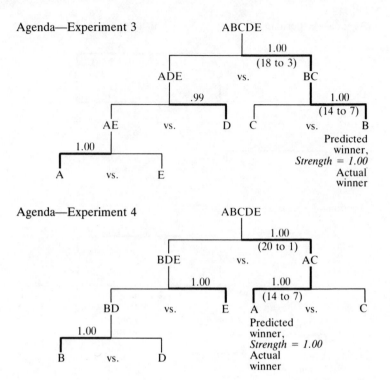

Agenda—Experiment 4

Key:

1.00 A boldface line with a value above it indicates that the set of alternatives at the end of the line has a strength of this value over the set of alternatives opposed to it.

(x to y) means that the decision went, as predicted, by a vote of x to y

[x to y] means that the decision went, contrary to prediction, by a vote of x to y

the chairman put the item to a vote, introduced the next item, and so on until an alternative was chosen.

The four agendas, shown in figure 1, were such that:

- the first was supposed to produce C, and did so;
- the second was supposed to produce D, but actually produced A;
- the third was supposed to produce B, and did so;
- the fourth was supposed to produce A, and did so.

Thus three out of four were, without question, correctly predicted. In the second experiment, the group was expected to produce D, but chose A, because, so Plott and Levine believe, a straw vote revealed E was the worst for everybody. This apparently changed the agenda to that of revised agenda 2 in figure 1 in which A is the predicted outcome. Whether one gives them credit for four out of four or three out of four, they still did remarkably well. The chance is less than 5 percent that three out of four of their predictions were correct by mere accident. That is, there is over a 95 percent probability that their predictions were correct because they truly controlled the outcome. Their experiments convince me, as I think they will convince you, that agenda control is really possible.

A NOTE ON MORALITY
Plott and Levine have been criticized—in my opinion, naively and improperly—for controlling or for trying to control the decision of the flying club. Given the absence of a general equilibrium of preferences, all agenda are biased toward one outcome or another. Even if they had wished, they could not have constructed an outcome-neutral agenda. Since they were required to choose some agenda, they might have chosen one biased toward or away from their preferred alternative. If one adopts an ethical standard requiring a choice biased toward the chooser, then they acted unexceptionally. If one adopts a standard requiring them to hurt themselves, then of course they are culpable. But is it not an odd standard to require a

man to act against himself? We do not apply such a standard to public men in their public acts. Indeed, we require the opposite, saying that they are poor and irresponsible statesmen if they do not choose an agenda biased in their favor. Should we use a different standard for private men in their private acts? We do not ask businessmen to price products so they will lose money. We do not ask litigants to present a weak case. It seems strange indeed, therefore, to ask an agenda committee to choose an agenda biased against its members. The benefits derived from the opportunity to control the agenda are, as Levine and Plott have remarked, no different from the benefits accruing from "political acumen, rhetorical skill, and knowledge of the preferences of group members." We do not ask the possessors of these skills to forego the benefits flowing therefrom and it seems equally unreasonable to ask members of an agenda committee to abandon their particular opportunities.

Looked at in another way, Plott and Levine acted in an exemplary fashion, conforming, so I believe, to the most demanding and restrictive moral standard. One of the earliest scholars to recognize that agendas, voting methods, and so on could always be manipulated to the advantage of one or another participant was the Reverend Charles L. Dodgson, otherwise known as Lewis Carroll. Remarking that strategic behavior "makes an election more a game of skill than a real test of the wishes of electors," his solution was not to condemn manipulation but rather to provide "that all should know the rules by which this game may be won." It seems to me that Plott and Levine, by studying agendas, by generalizing from their experience in the flying club, and by publishing their discoveries so that "all should know," acted exactly in accord with Dodgson's precept. Had they manipulated the decision and kept the knowledge to themselves, they would have satisfied conventional morality by doing the same as ordinary men. But they went further, much further. They revealed their action, studied how it was done, and showed other people how to do it, thereby offering a secret and a skill to all mankind, even though it might have been privately advantageous to keep it to themselves. Their actions ought not be condemned, but rather mightily praised.

Sources: The experimenters described their work in two essays: Michael E. Levine and Charles R. Plott, "Agenda Influence and Its Implications," *Virginia Law Review* 63, no. 4 (1977): 561–604, and Charles R. Plott and Michael E. Levine, "A Model of Agenda Influence on Committee Decisions," *American Economic Review* 68 (March 1978): 146–60. The quotation from Dodgson was first printed in Duncan Black, *The Theory of Committees and Elections* (Cambridge: Cambridge University Press, 1958), p. 182. Richard E. Freedman, my honors student at the University of Rochester, repeated this experiment with 11 students per group rather than 21. Amazingly, he obtained almost the same results, three out of four correct predictions, with one failure owing to an improperly allowed straw vote. See Richard E. Freedman, "On Using the Agenda to Influence Group Decisions," *Undergraduate Research Symposium* (Rochester, N.Y.: University of Rochester, April 13–14, 1976), p. 72.

4 GOUVERNEUR MORRIS IN THE PHILADELPHIA CONVENTION

For a disadvantaged politician, the main heresthetical problem is to attract supporters with whom he can turn his prospective loss into a realized win. There are at least two well-known solutions. One is the method of alliance, superficially a simple device, but practically difficult because it requires the invention of a proposal that otherwise strange bedfellows can mutually support. The other is the method of redefinition of the political situation so that formerly unsympathetic competitors wish to stand with the erstwhile disadvantaged. Redefinition, as carried out, for example, by the Whig-Republicans of the 1840s and 1850s, is probably even more difficult than alliance. Like alliance, redefinition depends in part on the invention of a new viewpoint, but it also requires rhetorical success in persuading indifferent people to accept the novelty. Yet difficult as both alliance and redefinition are, they are the ordinary ploys in the heresthetician's bag of tricks, used daily, simultaneously, and in various combinations.

Much of the time, furthermore, the heresthetician is in a hurry. Prospective winners need wait for no one and it is in their interest to push decisions to a hasty end. For the disadvantaged politician, therefore, heresthetical ploys must be devised and executed quickly. Hence the heresthetician is a battlefield strategist, an opportunist, not a closet planner and ideologue.

As an example of how alliance and redefinition appear in the fast-moving rough-and-tumble of legislative life, I will recount the history, in the Federal Convention of 1787, of the invention and adoption of the constitutional provisions for the electoral college. This is an especially interesting example because, over the course of three months, the delegates completely reversed themselves. At the beginning of the convention the delegates, voting by states, favored, by a vote of 8–2, a provision for the national legislature to elect the national executive. But near the end of the convention, they rejected this method by a vote of 2–8, with one state divided, adopting instead, by a vote of 9–2, the provision for election by the electoral college.

The master heresthetician in this dramatic reversal seems to have been Gouverneur Morris. Though now mostly forgotten, he was a dominant figure in the convention. Indeed, he actually wrote the final version of the Constitution and we owe to him its grand and sonorous phrasing. Furthermore, as a participant, both on the floor and in committee, he had at least as much to do as did anyone else with the substance beneath the phrases. According to James Madison's *Notes,* which are daily precis of the debates, Morris spoke more frequently than anyone else, even though he was absent for the first third of the convention. Despite his political ideals that were an odd combination even for that era—he stood for the old Whig notion of aristocratic society and democratic government and simultaneously for the liberal ideal of free trade and free men, the most antislavery of all the framers—still the other delegates apparently respected him because they put him on committees more frequently, relative to expectations, than any other active delegate.

In 1787 Morris was thirty-five years old, clearly a self-assured man who expected to run things, a man born to be masterful but with sufficient handicaps to motivate him to demonstrate his mastery. He was, for example, well-born but from his father's second family so his inheritance was meager. Eventually he became rich enough to buy the family estate, Morrisania in the Bronx. He was a big, handsome man, but one arm was withered from a scalding as a child and one leg had been amputated below the knee because of a fall from a horse several years previously. Perhaps as a result he had the reputation of a Don Juan. He had served in Congress from New York, but his political career was blocked by the party of Governor Clinton, which stood for just about everything Mor-

ris abhorred. So he migrated to Pennsylvania where he flour-
ished in both politics and commerce as the protégé and partner
of Robert Morris (no relation), the Financier of the Revolution, the leader of the Republican party, and Washington's
host throughout the convention.

I think Gouverneur Morris must have been a charming fellow, witty, self-deprecating, intense but open-minded and un-
grudging, quick in thought and speech and doubtless impetu-
ous. Here is an anecdote which biographers of Washington say
is apocryphal but which has two independent oral traditions
and may have survived mainly for its portrayal of Morris: During the convention, Hamilton (age thirty) is said to have
wagered a dinner for ten that Morris (age thirty-five) would
not dare to greet Washington (age fifty-five and their mutual
patron) familiarly. So at the next reception, Morris put his arm
around Washington's shoulder, saying, "My dear General,
how happy I am to see you looking so well." Washington
stared hard at him, said nothing, and, in a gesture of distaste,
lifted his hand to remove Morris's. As for the wagered enter-
tainment, Morris is said to have remarked, doubtless with wry
good humor, while consuming his dinner, that he "paid
dearly" for it.

Enough of the man. Let us now observe the heresthetician.

In the Virginia plan, which served as the basis for discussion
in the convention and was ultimately the embryo of the Constitution, the national executive was to be elected by the national legislature. This feature reflected the pattern of the
whole plan, namely a sharp separation between the proposed
federal government and the state governments. The lower
house of the federal legislature was to be selected directly by
citizens. The upper house was to be selected by the lower
house, and the executive and judiciary were to be selected by
the two houses together. Thus, the national government was
to be entirely separate electorally from the states and, furthermore, the national legislature was to be empowered to abro-
gate state laws. Had the Virginia plan been adopted without
amendment, the states would now be wholly subordinate

units, in an even weaker position than villages are vis-à-is their states.

The underlying motivation for this extreme nationalism was the conviction that the states governed badly and should be supervised by a national elite. The case against the states was probably best made by Madison, the main author of the Virginia plan, in a private manuscript (April 1787), "Vices of the Political System of the United States." Madison blamed the extreme weakness of the federal government on the failure of the states to pay requisitions, on their encroachments on federal authority, and on their refusal to carry out the provisions of the peace treaty of 1783, thereby risking another war with Britain. To explain the immediate economic and political crises of 1787, he blamed the states for their parochialism (e.g., beggaring their neighbors with trade restrictions), for their majority tyranny (e.g., favoring creditors with paper money, etc.), and for their inability to enforce laws (e.g., as in Shay's rebellion in Massachusetts in 1786, the crisis which, more than any other, shocked state legislators themselves and influenced them to send delegates to Philadelphia). Beneath all this substantive criticism was an elitist view of state legislatures whose mistakes, Madison thought, derived "from the sphere of life from which most of their members are called."

In the "Vices" Madison doubtless spoke for all the Virginian delegates, certainly for his close friend McClurg and for Washington, whose letters from this period are full of the same themes, and almost certainly also for Edmund Randolph and George Mason, who are often quoted in Madison's *Notes* with contemptuous references to state governments, especially state legislatures.

Furthermore, most of the other delegates shared Virginians' distaste for state governments. Of the 55 delegates, only five or six could be regarded as genuine anti-Federalists, that is, wholehearted supporters of provincial political establishments. These were Yates and Lansing of New York, who, however, went home July 10; Mercer of Maryland, who showed up for only two weeks in August; Luther Martin of Maryland, who was just about the only persistent anti-Federal voice during most of the Convention; and Elbridge Gerry of Massachusetts, who, while active all summer (29 May–17 September) in perfecting the Constitution, nevertheless refused to sign it and opposed its ratification. Perhaps one should also count George Mason of Virginia; but he is an equivocal case because he truly despised state governments and supported the extreme nationalism of the Virginia plan right up to the end of the convention. Still, he refused to sign the Constitution and opposed it in the Virginia ratifying convention, mainly because of highly parochial economic concerns that emerged late in August. Sometimes also Edmund Randolph of Virginia is called anti-Federalist because he also refused to sign out of the same economic parochialism. But I do not count him because he shared Madisonian nationalism and supported the Constitution in the Virginia ratifying convention.

Aside from these five or six, then, every other delegate who stayed to the end, and probably most of those who went home early, either had Federalist sympathies to begin with or acquired them during the summer. (For example, Rufus King came to Philadelphia a bit suspicious about the goal of the convention, but he was quickly converted to extreme nationalism by friends like Hamilton, Madison, and Morris. In a sense, King was the most Federalist of all because he was the last Federalist candidate for president in 1816.) Even the small state die-hards, who fought for a role for state legislatures in electing the Senate, cared very little about the state governments themselves. They simply wanted to ensure that states would be treated equally, to protect Connecticut and New Jersey against New York, Delaware against Pennsylvania, Maryland against Virginia, and so on. As Charles Pinckney of South Carolina predicted, cynically and quite correctly, "Give New Jersey an equal vote, and she will dismiss her scruples, and concur on the National system."

To summarize bluntly, most of the delegates were predisposed to favor the Virginia plan as a device to bring uninformed and myopic state officials under the control of a national elite, like the delegates themselves. They persisted in favoring the plan largely in accord with their dispositions. Some democratic

New Englanders (e.g., Roger Sherman of Connecticut and Rufus King of Massachusetts) were not much attracted to the Virginian electoral methods to begin with and shifted to alternative methods easily, while some highly elitist Southerners (like George Mason of Virginia, Hugh Williamson of North Carolina, and John Rutledge and Charles Pinckney of South Carolina) remained devoted right up to the end of the convention to the idea of electing the executive in the national legislature.

But this method was opposed from the very beginning, especially by Pennsylvanians. They were just as federalist as Madison, but they had different expectations about how election in the legislature would work. They attributed the vices of the state governments to legislative supremacy, not merely to provinciality. They agreed with Madison that state legislators tended to be uninformed, reckless, and myopic, back-country demagogues. But the Pennsylvanians thought the worse problem was that the legislatures were unrestrained.

From this diagnosis it follows that the appropriate constitutional structure is a thoroughgoing separation of powers. Not only should the federal government be separated from the states, as in the Virginia plan, but within the federal government the several parts should be independent from each other. James Wilson of Pennsylvania, proposing the popular election of the executive, said he "wished to derive not only both branches of the Legislature from the people, without the intervention of State Legislatures, but the Executive also; in order to make them as independent as possible from each other, as well as of the States."

This is, of course, what was eventually achieved with the electoral college in 1787 and the Seventeenth Amendment in 1912. But in July of 1787, about the only people with this vision were the Pennsylvanians, especially Wilson and G. Morris, who believed local radicals in Pennsylvania exploited the unicameral legislature and weak executive. Because the opponents of this unchecked legislature believed it encouraged demagoguery, the Pennsylvanian Constitution had become the center of partisan dispute in the state, so central in fact that the populist party was called "Constitutionalist" while the lib-

eral anti-Constitution party was called "Republican." Most of
the Pennsylvanian delegates were strong Republicans, and
they had no wish to reproduce in the federal government the
populist defects they despised at home. Hence they favored
some kind of separation of powers, and I will from now on call
their position "separationist."

The first alternative the separationists offered to the Virginia
plan was popular election. Although it gained some support
over the summer, it was too bizarre an idea to be accepted.
Wilson (Pa.) recognized this when he first brought it up early in
June, saying he was "almost unwilling to declare" his preference because he was "apprehensive that it might appear chi-
merical." And indeed it did. Mason (Va.) seems to have spoken
for nearly everybody when he said: "It would be as unnatural to
refer the choice of a Chief Magistrate to the people, as it would,
to refer a trial of colours to a blind man." Consequently, once
they recognized that popular election could not win, the separationists altered their attack, heresthetically manipulating the
perception of the issue and simultaneously and opportunisti-
cally searching for allies.

The time frame in which the separationists had to work was
as follows. On July 17, they learned with certainty that popular election would not work when, during consideration of the
Virginia plan as revised in the Committee of the Whole, Morris's motion for election by "citizens" failed 1–9, with only
Pennsylvania voting aye. Their first chance (stage 1) at reori-
entation was then the nine days from July 17 to July 26, before
the revised Virginia plan was referred to the Committee on
Detail. Their second chance (stage 2) came on August 24
when the convention considered the relevant part of the report
of the Committee on Detail. Since they were able to generate
a deadlock on August 24, they had a third chance (stage 3) in
the Committee on Postponed Matters which reported September 4–5.

In stage 1 the separationists' first tactic was to discredit legislative election. In eighteenth-century political philosophy, the
fundamental argument for the separationists' position was
(from Montesquieu) the doctrine that liberty depended on the

separation of powers. As applied here, this was the proposition, in Morris's words: "If the Executive be chosen by the National Legislature, he will not be independent on it; and if not independent, usurpation and tyranny on the part of the Legislature will be the consequence." Such inference of appropriate institutions from philosophical doctrine is persuasive to philosophers—Madison, for example, was easily converted to the separationists' position, apparently by the philosophical argument alone, and in his hands it was fashioned into one of the main tenets of our constitutional tradition. But philosophical abstractions are probably less persuasive for men of affairs, so for them the separationists had a different tactic—namely, to associate legislative election with features of political life that the supporters of legislative election themselves agreed were bad. Hence Morris and Wilson reiterated that legislative election implied "intrigue" or, in Morris's words, "cabal and corruption." By "intrigue" they meant the formation of coalitions prior to parliamentary votes of confidence to unseat one cabinet and put in another. Of course, this is accepted practice now, but in the eighteenth century such maneuvers seemed to put office above principle and were shocking even to supporters of legislative election—Mason, for example, was the first one to mention "intrigue" in legislative election. Hence the association that Morris emphasized could be believed and was indeed eventually believed by nearly everybody, an elegant heresthetic maneuver. Having once obtained general agreement, even from people like Roger Sherman of Connecticut and Rufus King of Massachusetts who were not initially fearful of intrigue, the separationists used the agreement about intrigue to discredit legislative election and replace it with the electoral college.

Of course, saying—indeed repeating and repeating—that legislative election implies "intrigue" does not make it so, nor does it necessarily convince anyone. The separationists needed a heresthetical device to dramatize the association. This they found in the proposition: "If elected by the legislature, then the executive should (1) have a long term and (2) be ineligible for reelection, in order to avoid intrigue at the second election and, simultaneously, to give him time to learn his job; on the other hand, if not elected by the legislature, he might have a short term and stand often for reelection in customary democratic fashion." In a series of three motions on July 17, just after the rejection of Morris's motion for popular election, the separationists managed to imprint this proposition indelibly.

It was voted unanimously that the executive "be chosen by the National Legislature," so it was in order to consider "for a term of seven years." Houstoun (Ga.) moved, Morris seconded, and the convention unanimously agreed to postpone the motion on the length of the term. Next in regular order came "to be ineligible a second time," which Houstoun moved to delete, Sherman (Conn.) seconded, and Morris supported with the argument that ineligibility "destroyed the great motive to good behavior," as if saying to him, "make hay while the sun shines." So ineligibility was deleted, 6–4. Then, taking up the postponed motion, McClurg (Va.) moved and Morris seconded to strike out "seven years" and insert "good behavior." This failed, 4–6, but it certainly got the point across.

Implying, as it did, life tenure, it shocked McClurg's Virginia colleagues, especially since Washington was the only serious candidate. Mason sharply rebuked McClurg and Madison (now a separationist) defended his parliamentarily inexperienced friend, showing that the motion embodied the separation of powers, even though it might not be the "proper" expedient. The main effect of McClurg's motion was to embed "intrigue" in the Virginia plan: if legislative election meant repeated episodes of intrigue, then the best way to eliminate them was life tenure. From then on, every time the method of election was considered, if the convention adopted legislative election, then it added "seven years" and "ineligibility"; while if it adopted another kind of electoral system, then it also adopted a shorter term and allowed reeligibility.

The motions by Houstoun and McClurg were clearly heresthetical. The reversal of consideration of length of term first and ineligibility second to ineligibility first and length of term second was necessary to delete ineligibility. Almost certainly, in regular order with a long term adopted first, ineligibility would not have been deleted. Hence, Houstoun's motions were essential in order to force people to consider ineligibility on its own merits. (This may be all that Houstoun intended, but from Morris's intimate involvement in all three motions, I suspect it was a planned sequence. If not, then Morris even more cleverly exploited McClurg's innocence and Houstoun's simple intention.) Once it appeared likely that the term would be short and hence admit "intrigue" at each election, it was heresthetically appropriate to move, as McClurg did, "good behavior" in order to minimize "intrigue."

Madison tells us that McClurg's motion was not serious but merely "to enforce the argument," and that the vote on McClurg's motion was "not to be considered as any certain index of opinion [i.e., in favor of good behavior], as a number in the affirmative probably had it chiefly in view to alarm those attached to a dependence of the Executive or the Legislative and thereby to facilitate some final arrangements of a contrary tendency." The "avowed friends' of good behavior were, he said, no more than three or four, yet four supporting states required at least ten delegates' votes. Clearly, at least six delegates—including Madison himself—voted contrary to their true tastes in order to bring about an advantageous parliamentary situation to "facilitate . . . contrary . . . arrangements."

I think the heresthetical device was successful. Two days later, in the course of urging another method, Wilson, complacently and rather slyly—for he was one of the architects of the separationists' rhetoric—observed: "It seems to be the unanimous sense that the Executive should not be appointed by the Legislature, unless he is rendered ineligible a 2d. time." To the degree that Wilson was correct about unanimity, the heresthetic had succeeded at least in rendering the method in the Virginia plan dubious.

Brilliant as was the heresthetical tactic, it was not enough to win. The separationists also needed allies and, once the theme of intrigue was fully elaborated, they found their allies among the delegates from the small states.

On the surface, this was a strange place to look. Just a few days earlier, on July 16, the convention had adopted equal representation of states in the Senate. This was doubtless the most important action of the whole summer because it satisfied the delegates of the small states and kept them in attendance. Had they gone home, the chance for unification would have been lost, perhaps forever. But at the same time it was a terrible blow to the hopes of both Virginians and Pennsylvanians who had come to the convention determined to eliminate the equality of states, which they believed was the most unfair feature of the government under the Articles. In the end, on July 16, Pennsylvania and Virginia and South Carolina had collapsed in the face of the terrible determination of Paterson (N.J.), Ellsworth (Conn.), Bedford (Del.), et al. that the interest of small states be protected. Still as late as July 17 Morris by himself tried to keep the fight going, although everyone else recognized that the fight was over, and Madison privately recorded his own quiet sympathy with Morris's lonely and quixotic stand. This is why the alliance of separationists and small states seems so strange.

Later in the morning of July 17 came Houstoun's motions, which nevertheless resulted in the reaffirmation of legislative election. But on July 19 Morris again opened up the subject and Paterson, perhaps still euphoric over his great victory on July 16, moved to substitute election by electors rather than the national legislature. In his plan the small states would be overrepresented in the selection of electors, and so his motion in a sense continued the battle over the Senate. But this time it was no battle because the separationists immediately recognized the advantage it gave them. Virginia (now mostly separationist under Madison's influence) and Pennsylvania voted right along with the small states. Thereafter Paterson and Ellsworth did not need to take the lead in promoting the electoral college because Morris, letting bygones be bygones, joined— and indeed led—his old enemies to a new victory.

On July 19 the separationist–small state coalition won, but on July 24 yet another dimension was added to the dispute and legislative election was again adopted and finally confirmed on July 26. This new dimension was the cost to peripheral states of sending electors to a capital somewhere in the Middle Atlantic states. Today we think this an odd concern. But in 1787 the delegates from New Hampshire did not get to Philadelphia until the middle of the summer owing to a failure of the state legislature to appropriate funds for travel; and the state of Georgia had so much difficulty maintaining delegates at both Philadelphia for the Convention and New York for the Congress that its delegates were required to travel back and forth between the two. This new consideration attracted not only the peripheral states (Ga., N.H.) but also some of the small states hitherto most devoted to the small-state interest (N.J., Del.). These delegations, together with the core of the party in favor of legislative election (N.C., S.C., Mass.), were of course enough to affirm legislative election on July 26, and it was then incorporated into the first draft of the Constitution produced by the Committee on Detail (July 27–August 6).

It might be supposed that this finished the matter. But the separationists had not really had their day in court. Although Wilson had argued their case in June, it was not until Morris took up the cause on July 17 that they were brought together as a coherent group. So in a sense Morris was anticipating and prepared for his second chance on August 24, when, in the regular order of review of the draft constitution from the Committee on Detail, the provisions for choosing the executive came up.

Immediately, John Rutledge of South Carolina moved that when the legislature elected the executive, it do so by a joint ballot of the two houses. Rutledge had been a diehard opponent of the equality of states in the upper house and a joint ballot would, in part, erase that equality. The 26-member upper house would be outvoted by the 65-member lower house. Unfortunately for Rutledge, who was a strong and consistent supporter of legislative election, the very act of moderating the equality of states exposed the method of election to heresthetical manipulation by Gouverneur Morris. Had Rutledge not moved anything, Morris might never have had his second chance. But Rutledge did move for a joint ballot and Morris reactivated the coalition of small states and separationists, a coalition which had been successful on July 19 and then unsuccessful on July 24.

Delegates from New Jersey and Connecticut responded vigorously to Rutledge's motion. They had been the leaders of the small states in the fight over representation in the upper house, and naturally they were upset by this oblique attack on the position they thought they had previously settled forever. Despite, however, the objections of Ellsworth (Conn.) and Dayton (N.J.), Rutledge's motion passed, 7–4, with even two small states supporting. Dayton immediately moved that each state have a single vote on the joint ballot. This would of course restore the equality that Rutledge's motion had upset. Dayton's motion failed, 5–6, but it obtained the vote of all the small states except New Hampshire, whose delegates had not been present for the great battle over equality in the upper house and were not, therefore, as sensitive as the delegates from other small states to the significance of the joint ballot. Still, even in failing, Dayton's motion signaled to everyone that the small-state coalition had been reborn. Morris, ever the parliamentary opportunist, observed and responded. He moved immediately for electing the executive by popularly elected electors. This, too, failed 5–6; but it reunited the core of the small states and the core of the separationists. Dayton then moved to postpone, which also failed; and Jacob Broome of Delaware moved to refer the whole question to a committee, which failed by a tie. Morris renewed the attack with a motion for electors themselves to be chosen in some unspecified way. This substantive motion also obtained a tie, 4–4, with two states divided and one temporarily absent. A tie on a substantive motion is, of course, a serious matter, so Dayton again moved to postpone and this time his motion was accepted. Soon thereafter a committee on postponed matters was chosen and this was the main business assigned to it.

Thus Morris and Dayton, by a kind of ping-pong of motions, achieved what Morris, at least, had wanted all along—namely, a full reconsideration of the method of election. It was the tie vote that did it. The men of 1787 did not understand about voting cycles, but they did know what is, for practical life,

sufficient: that a tie on a substantive motion necessitates re-
working the substantive content. In addition, we can now see
something that they did not quite understand. Let:

a stand for "legislative election without joint ballot";
b stand for "election by electors";
c stand for "legislative election with joint ballot."

Then, observe:

a beat *b* (on July 24);
b tied with *c* (on August 24);
c beat *a* (on August 24).

So, by inference, electors were preferred to legislative election
on August 24 (i.e., *b* tied *c* beat *a,* or *b* beat *a*). But still on
July 24, legislative election was directly preferred to electors,
and again legislative election was supported against, presumably, all comers in the vote on Rutledge's motion on August 24.
Whether one understands the significance of cycles or not, it is
clear that there was confusion in the results of the Dayton-
Morris ping-pong. Rutledge should never have brought up the
joint ballot.

Although the delegates voted by states when they voted on
motions, they may have voted as individuals when they chose
committees. At least, that seems to be the only way that one
can explain the formation of a committee on postponed matters that was stacked in favor of the separationist position. The
large number of separationist and small-state delegates from
Pennsylvania and Delaware produced a committee of eleven
(one from each state) such that each member was the one
from his state most favorable to the separationist position. G.
Morris (Pa.) and Madison (Va.) were the two most vocal separationists. King (Mass.), Dickinson (Del.), and Carroll (Md.)
had usually supported the separationists when others from
their states had not. Sherman (Conn.) and Brearly (N.J.)
were, on August 26, the main spokesmen for the small-state
interest. From the other states, uniformly, the least hostile to
the separationist position were chosen: from New Hampshire,
Gilman rather than Langdon, who had actually spoken for the

joint ballot; from Georgia, Baldwin rather than Few, who never spoke (according to Madison's *Notes*); from North Carolina, Williamson rather than Spaight, who had seconded Houstoun; and from South Carolina, Butler rather than Rutledge or Charles Pinckney, both of whom had strongly supported legislative election.

A committee stacked like this, of course, produced a separationist result. It was a plan for an electoral college tailored to satisfy all those who might conceivably be persuaded to oppose legislative choice of the executive. For those in favor of popular election—the hard core of the separationists—electors were to be chosen in a manner prescribed by state legislatures, which thus did not preclude popular election. For the distant states, the electors of each state were to meet in the state capital, not in the national capital. Thus the electoral college would not meet, its members would merely ballot. Finally, for the small states there were two provisions: The college was to have as many electors from each state as the state had senators and representatives, which provision gave the small states a slight edge. And, if no candidate had a majority in the college, the Senate (wherein states were equal) was to choose from the five highest.

It is unclear just what the framers expected about election in the Senate. I think that those who wanted the legislature to elect expected that the Senate would usually do so, while those who opposed legislative election thought it would seldom occur. If so, there was a systematic bias in favor of the committee plan, each person seeing in it what was preferred by him.

The committee plan survived on the floor without substantial change, except to relocate the residual power to elect from the Senate to the House, voting by states. This minor change preserved the advantage for small states and satisfied those who thought the Senate might become too powerful. Rutledge did try to substitute legislative election for the electoral college, but this failed, 2–8, with one state divided. The convention then adopted the report of the committee (for the college) by a vote of 9–2, completely reversing thereby the initial endorsement in June of the method in the Virginia plan.

So the committee plan stuck. It was put together over a weekend to satisfy diverse, parochial, and temporary interests; but, with only the minor modification of the Twelfth Amendment, it has served adequately for two centuries. It may be that this is mere luck. But it is just as possible that the electoral college system worked because it was the clear expression, even though hastily devised, of the idea of the separation of powers, which is the fundamental principle of Western constitutionalism.

We do not, of course, know how this compromise was made, but it seems almost certain that Gouverneur Morris dominated the committee. From Madison we know that, even though Brearly (N.J.) served as the chairman, Morris acted as spokesman, at least on the plan for the electoral college. Thus, when Randolph (Va.) and C. Pinckney (S.C.) asked for an explanation of the committee draft, Morris responded, "giving the reasons of the committee and his own." And when Wilson (Pa.) criticized the plan for giving too much power to the Senate, Morris "expressed his wonder at the observations of Mr. Wilson." Just beneath the surface of Madison's emotionless precis we can sense Morris's sharp resentment, as a proud and offended author, that his separationist ally James Wilson, who was indeed the original separationist, should fail to give unquestioning support to Morris's workable construction. Since Morris acted, in these two ways, very much like an author, I conclude that he is the one who put together the committee plan and to whom therefore we are indebted for the electoral college.

We are indebted to Morris for more than the committee plan. Of course, all the people who voted for the plan and who at one stage or another helped it along are causal forces for the college. This category includes all of the at least 23 delegates necessary for a majority in the nine supporting delegations (and perhaps as many as 31 delegates from those states). Furthermore, it includes among those who went home early, Paterson (N.J.), who first suggested the small-state interest in electors, and Ellsworth (Conn.), who pushed the idea along, McClurg (Va.) and Houstoun (Ga.), who served perhaps as Morris's foils, and even Rutledge (S.C.), who unwittingly gave Morris and Dayton a chance. But throughout the event persists the figure of Morris, the opportunistic heresthetician.

Perhaps his most interesting feature is precisely his opportunism. Morris had no plan in the sense of an antecedently worked out strategy then more or less mechanically applied. All he had was an idea—namely, the separation of powers— and its practical goal in this situation: to eliminate the selection of the executive by the legislature. Working with these concerns uppermost, he was otherwise flexible. Doubtless he, like Wilson, would have preferred popular election, but when it failed and when the opportunity arose to ally with small-state interests for a college, Morris unhesitatingly allied, on July 19, on August 24, and in the committee. And as is apparent in his ping-pong of motions with Dayton on August 24, he was wholly willing to do so in order to win. Wilson and Madison, on the other hand, showed less interest in speedy floor compromises and for that reason were probably less influential on the outcome.

The same kind of quick floor management is observable in Morris's manipulation of "intrigue" on July 17 and his search for inconsistency on August 24. I think the series of motions with Houstoun and McClurg about ineligibility and length of term may have been planned in the sense that Morris suggested them to the movers, probably on the morning or during the day of the motions, saying he would back them up, as he then did. On the other hand, even these motions may not have been planned; but since Morris seems to have seen from the beginning just where they would lead, we can say at least that he took quick advantage of them, pushing them hard and drawing out their implications, so much so that Wilson could remark two days later about the "unanimous sense" that legislative election implied ineligibility for a second term.

While the Houstoun-McClurg series may have been planned, clearly the Dayton-Morris series on August 24 was not. After Rutledge's motion for a joint ballot was adopted, Dayton immediately moved "each state having one vote," which failed, and soon thereafter Morris moved election by the people. Immediately after it failed, Dayton moved to postpone, which failed, leading to Broome's motion to refer, which lost by a tie. Then immediately Morris moved election by electors, which failed by a tie. And immediately thereafter came a postponement "at the instance," Madison tells us, "of Deputies of New Jersey" (presumably Dayton). I doubt very much if these seven motions consumed more than an hour. For most of them Madison records no debate, and indeed most of them are procedural so that no debate was necessary or appropriate. So this whole proceeding, which was so crucial to the postponement and the the appointment of the committee on postponed matters, could not have been planned. Rather it was improvised, each motion exploiting the situation generated by the previous one and leading coherently to a situation that the next motion could exploit. This is, it seems to me, the height of the heresthetician's art, the ability to shift from moment to moment, poking and pushing the world until it favors the heresthetician's cause.

Perhaps this is why it is so difficult to generalize about the heresthetician's art. It is experimental, because, if any expedient fails, he goes on immediately to the next. It is often fleeting, a quick foray, intuitively designed, not a deeply well-worked out plan. But there do seem to be some regularities in it. The heresthetician thrives when he is losing because he is driven, it seems, by an intense desire to win. This is what inspires his creativity and this is why a person like Morris is heresthetically adept. And the creativity itself seems to consist of recombining the world, as in this event, making an alliance of exceedingly strange bedfellows, searching for statements that lead to incoherence and thus delay, and attaching new meanings to old ideas, as "cabal and corruption" were attached to legislative election. And most of all, given the persona and the nature of the creativity, there is an aura of opportunism over it all.

Sources. All the quotations in this chapter are from Max Farrand, ed., *The Records of the Federal Convention of 1787,* rev. ed., 4 vols. (New Haven: Yale University Press, 1911, 1937, and 1964). A more detailed version of this story is in William H. Riker, "The Heresthetic of Constitution-Making: The Presidency in 1787, with Comments on Determinism and Rational Choice," *American Political Science Review* 78 (March 1984): 1–16.

5 HERESTHETIC IN FICTION

Novelists hardly ever write about political events. Sometimes they do develop their subjects' characters against a political background, but even then the plots and stories are not about politics, but about love affairs, wars, getting ahead and decaying, marriage and divorce, trickery, violence, seduction, thievery, retribution, salvation, and so on. There is good reason for this. Politics is winning and losing, which depend, mostly, on how large and strong one side is relative to the other. The actions of politics consist in making agreements to join people in alliances and coalitions—hardly the stuff to release readers' adrenalin as do seductions, quarrels, or chases. Still the neglect of politics in novels is unfortunate because good opportunities are missed. As Greek dramatists and Shakespeare demonstrated, political ambition, and indeed political success, uniquely reveal tragic flaws in character and give rise to the sin of pride, thus allowing the dramatist to depict retribution.

At least one novelist, however, has recognized the literary potential of politics. He is C. P. Snow, whose novel *The Masters* is, so far as I know, the only one in which politics is not mere background but the very plot itself. Deservedly, *The Masters* made Snow's reputation. Some critics have failed to recognize it as a political novel because it is simply about an election in a college. But college politics are intense—bitter, as it is said, because so little is at stake. In Snow's story about making coalitions, pride and ambition and humiliation and failure are displayed against a background of political bitterness that renders them both necessary and poignant.

The event in *The Masters* is simple enough. Fellows in a Cambridge college learn that their Master is dying of cancer.

During his protracted illness, they form coalitions to elect his successor. One is for Jago, a warm, impulsive, proud, and uneasy man, lacking self-confidence and sympathetically concerned about his colleagues, even his enemies. The other is for Crawford, a cool, self-contained, self-confident, and arrogant man, not much interested in other people. Jago, fifty, is a humanist and a Tory, "not so distinguished academically." Crawford, fifty-six, is "one of the best biologists alive," and politically left, which in 1936 means being opposed to the spread of fascism, especially to Franco. The story is told from the point of view of Lewis Eliot who, though on the left, is committed to Jago because he likes Jago's imagination and sympathy and thinks Crawford is "devastatingly sensible," "impervious," and without "a scrap of imagination." The main protagonists are college politicians par excellence: Brown, who is committed to Jago out of long friendship, and Chrystal, who is committed to Jago only out of his friendship with Brown. They form a coalition for Jago and it is apparently successful at first. But gradually it crumbles, and in the end Crawford is elected, 7-6, with Chrystal switching to support him the day before the ballot. Altogether there are four switches and an appropriate dramatic climax in each one. Chrystal's switch is, however, definitive, so that his is the most interesting politically.

This plot enables Snow to depict a character whose merits and defects might not be easily appreciated in another setting. Even more, it enables him to display retribution not as divine decision but as a part of the natural order of the world. Jago yearns for the glory of office—for himself, to reassure himself, and for his wife, to gratify and strengthen her. He wants the glory so much that he does things shameful in his own eyes in the hope of winning. In the end, Jago's wife is excruciatingly humiliated, and he himself is no longer sure who his friends are, or, indeed, if he has any.

Here one sees the value of the political plot. In politics, when the proud are humbled, they are humbled by the very act that reveals their pride. This may, as some have said, seem to mystics a banal moralism. But it is in fact true that the structure of society at once provokes pride and rebukes the proud. This truth of nature requires a political setting and a political plot, and this is why it is worth taking the politics in Snow's novel seriously. To grasp the moral, one must understand the politics, which I intend to elucidate here.

If we read superficially, the political theme is the contest between Jago's supporters and Crawford's supporters about which one would be the better Master. Since, however, both are adequate, this does not appear to be a profound issue. But I have found that it deeply engages readers and they take sides readily. For many years I have amused myself by recording the votes of other readers, mostly college professors. Jago has won hands down, mainly, I suppose, because most professors would like to have a warm and concerned president (or better, dean or chairman—for, in American terms, that is what the Master would be). But having served under a variety of decanal and presidential personalities, give me the Crawfords of this world every time. The Crawfords manage the organization efficiently and for the general good and, unlike the Jagos, they will not tolerate human sentiment or the impulsiveness that endangers it. Chrystal sensed this difference, which was part of his motive for defection. Knowing what I do now, after forty years in academe, brings me down on Crawford's side from the start, although I must confess that thirty years ago I liked Jago best, just as the young men in the novel do.

To read a bit more deeply than the mere contest between candidates, the story is about ordinary political events, namely wooing supporters. While the description of this routine is fascinating, perhaps because it is seldom depicted, merely building a coalition is not heresthetic. The assembling of persons already convinced doubtless requires care and tact, but it does not require the essential heresthetical skill of transforming the situation from unfavorable to favorable.

Both the coalitions in the novel were, however, built the easy way. Eliot is inclined to regard Brown as a fine political manager. But Brown is really an order-taker, not a salesman. The only adherent he brings into his coalition is Chrystal, who later defects. As can be seen in the righthand column of table 1,

TABLE 1
Members of the Two Coalitions

Name	Academic Field	Age	Politics	Reasons for Favoring Candidate
(*For Crawford*)				
Getliffe	Physics	34	Left	"master . . . must be a distinguished scholar" (p. 77) Jago is an "absurd conservative" (p. 78)
*Nightingale	Chemistry	43	Unknown	envy, perhaps wanted to be like Crawford (p. 161)
*Chrystal	Classics	48	Right	"Crawford will make a good master" (p. 343)
Winslow	Classics	63	Radical	dislike of Jago (p. 19)
Despard-Smith	Classics	70	Right	Crawford's "made a name for himself" (p. 324) and "a tinge of sadic warmth" in distressing his friend Jago (p. 325)
*Pilbrow	Classics	74	Left	"I can't vote for Jago. I can't vote for someone who won't throw his weight on our side" (p. 246)
(*For Jago*)				
Luke	Physics	24	Left	"Jago would make one of the best Masters this college has ever had" (p. 107)
Calvert	Oriental studies	27	Center	Jago's "not commonplace," Crawford's "too complacent" (p. 53)
Eliot	Law	32	Left	Jago's sympathy and imaginativeness
Brown	History	46	Right	affection for Jago (p. 57)
*Gay	Norse myth	80	Unknown	respect for judgment of Calvert and Eliot (p. 295)

*Indicates switchers

Luke, Calvert, Eliot, and Brown himself choose Jago because they liked his character. The sole convert to Jago's side is Gay, old and forgetful and incredibly vain—he boasts often of his fourteen honorary degrees. Initially, he preferred Crawford for reasons never specified. When Calvert and Eliot seek to convert him, however, he converts easily, though it is not clear whether he does so because he trusts the judgment of the young men or because he is delighted to possess (as he thinks) the casting vote.

Crawford's coalition was built the same easy way. It did not even have a manager. Winslow convened it simply out of hatred for Jago. But Winslow has no particular affection for Crawford either. Of all the fellows, Winslow alone is willing to let the selection go to the Visitor (a bishop), as it would if neither candidate got an absolute majority. Nevertheless, close to indifferent though he is, he stays with Crawford all the way. So does Despard-Smith, though he is equally ambiguous. He admires Crawford's academic success but despises him as a "bolshevik"—actually a middle-class Labourite. Despard-Smith likes Jago well enough, but he is a disappointed old man, a secret drunkard, who feels used and discarded by the college. He also feels a "sadic warmth" in bringing the same disappointment to a man he actually likes. On the other hand, Getliffe thinks Crawford the best on all counts, for his scientific achievements and for his political stand.

These three come to Crawford right away without being asked. So eventually do his other three supporters, but they take longer to find their way to him. Nightingale, a chemist, had been an innovator in his youth. Then his creativity dried up and he lived on in the vain hope of recognition. He envied and hated the successful Crawford and so initially favored Jago. Desperate for notice, he asked Jago to promise to appoint him Tutor and Jago deceitfully sought, evidently without success, to assure Nightingale that he had a chance. Then, in a bizarre reversal just as he was passed over again for the Royal Society, he fastened on Crawford as a hero. From then on Nightingale became the most ardent member of the Crawford party, circulating malicious gossip about Jago and his wife.

The second shift to Crawford is made by Pilbrow. He had been a fine classicist and now is an aging literary party-goer and patron in Cambridge and in Europe. By every count of personality, temperament, and style except ideology, he is for Jago. But in the end, he cares more about European politics than college politics. So he switches from Jago to Crawford as a statement against fascism.

The final switch to Crawford is by Chrystal on the day before the election. Chrystal initiates the move without solicitation by Crawford or by any manager for Crawford. Consequently it can be said that both coalitions were built up almost entirely by the private decisions of the fellows and not by logrolling or reconsiderations heresthetically generated. There is one possible exception: Gay, with his vanity prompted by Eliot, may have switched just for the chance to have the casting vote, certainly a new and private issue. He got his chance to do so, however, without switching, simply by withdrawing from the coalition for Crawford. Thus rendered apparently decisive, he could vote his true taste, which was, as it turned out, to accept the young men's preference for Jago. So it seems that all the votes were more or less freely cast.

This fact is displayed in figure 1. In this graph, each voter's taste is measured on two dimensions. One dimension is national and international politics, which surely counted much for Getliffe and Pilbrow. The other dimension is private judgments on the abilities and the personae of the two candidates. The combination for each fellow is represented as a point in the plane. Thus Eliot, who believed Jago best and who was politically left, is shown in the upper lefthand corner.

That Crawford won is displayed by the line H, which divides the majority from the minority. Since line H is not parallel to either axis, neither dimension of taste could by itself account for the outcome. On the other hand, two dimensions are sufficient to divide the group neatly. Since both dimensions were present from the beginning, this means that no heresthetician generated still a third dimension in order to confuse matters. Furthermore, since line H is straight, no one is strikingly out of place. This means that no bribery or logrolling took place.

FIGURE 1

Representation in Two-Dimensional Space of Fellows' Preferences
at Time of Ballot

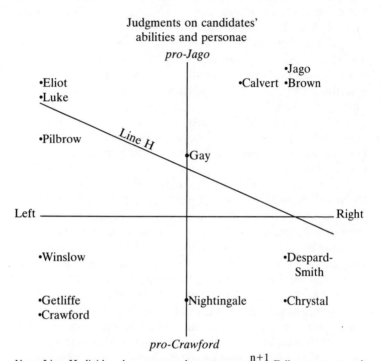

Note: Line H divides the space so that, at most, $\frac{n+1}{2}$ Fellows are on each
side. Crawford's coalition lies below and left of line H; Jago's above and right.
Snow does not specify a political position for either Gay or Nightingale. For
both, however, the political dimension is irrelevant, for Gay because he is
nearly senile, for Nightingale because his hatred of Jago and near adoration of
Crawford blot out everything else.

Suppose there had been a "corrupt bargain." On the day
before the election, after Chrystal had announced his switch,
Jago, in agony and shame, tried to bribe Chrystal. ("I'm
ready," Jago said, "to talk over all the practical arrangements
we can conceivably make for the future. . . .") Had Chrystal
accepted, even though now convinced that Crawford was bet-

though now convinced that Crawford was better, then line H
would have to go above the point for Despard-Smith, curve back
on itself, and drop vertically to take in Chrystal's point. But line
H is straight, and this is evidence that here are expressed the true
tastes of the fellows on these two dimensions, uncontaminated,
as it were, by logrolling or private deals.

Going beyond mere alignments and reading at the deepest
political level, this is a story about heresthetical manipulations.
They are the engine of retribution within the drama about
pride. It is a particularly interesting kind of heresthetic because it is entirely in the hands of one man. Indeed, in almost
every action more involved than taking sides, Chrystal is the
crucial figure and thus the agent for the outcome.

Eliot, the narrator, tries at the end to explain Chrystal's shift
and is torn between two interpretations. According to one,
Chrystal was irrational, moved "by vacillations he did not understand" and driven by an inexplicable "impulse to change
sides, to resent one's leader and become fascinated by one's
chief opponent." So Eliot concludes: "The more certain men
are that they are chasing their own concrete and 'realistic'
ends, so it often seemed to me, the more nakedly do you see
all the strands they could never give a reason for" (p. 338).

Alternatively, Eliot sets forth a second theory: that Chrystal
was in fact a rational realist. "He had his own sensible policy
for the college: that was safer with Crawford than Jago. . . .
He had come to think that, if Jago became Master, his own
policy and power would dwindle to nothing within the next
five years. . . . He was absolutely right" (pp. 338–39). From
this followed, quite reasonably, a vote for Crawford.

Which of Eliot's interpretations are we to accept? They are,
I believe, mutually exclusive, because in the former Chrystal
understands neither nature nor himself, while in the latter he
understands both very well and behaves rationally in light of
his understanding. It is only in this passage that Eliot is ambiguous about Chrystal's motives. Earlier in the novel everything
Eliot teels us about Chrystal leads to the second interpretation. Why, then, did Eliot attempt an explanation in terms of
irrationality only at the very end?

He was guilty, I believe, of exactly the same kind of faulty
and self-serving observation as most other theorists of the irrational. Eliot badly wanted Jago to win. Although initially he
was rather detached, as the coalition developed, as he himself
took a hand in the management of it by trying to persuade
Pilbrow, Despard-Smith, and Gay to switch, Eliot came to
identify closely with the coalition as a social organization. Its
purpose became his purpose and, when it failed, he fell into
the fallacy of egomorphism—that is, of structuring one's perception of others like one's perception of one's self. But politics does make strange bedfellows. The people in a coalition
share only its official purpose, and sometimes, as with Chrystal, not even that. The shift that appeared irrational given
Eliot's goals was realistic given Chrystal's. Of Eliot's two interpretations, therefore, I think we can discard the first as dis-
torted by his momentary pique. All the other information
Snow has allowed Eliot to give us confirms the second, ratio-
nalistic interpretation of Chrystal's behavior.

Early in the novel Eliot reflected on "three kinds of power."
Jago, he said, "longed to be first . . . for the trappings . . .
and show of power." Also, "he had dreams," and he told
Chrystal, "We can make a great college" (p. 67). Brown, on
the other hand, wanted only "to handle, coax, guide, contrive,
so that men found themselves in places he had designed; he
did not want an office . . . , it was good enough to . . . see it
work" (p. 66). Chrystal, as well, wanted no office, indeed
believed himself unqualified for high office, but he wanted "to
be known as a man of power." "Brown would have been
content to get Jago elected and influence him afterwards," but
"Chrystal was impelled to have his own part recognized by
Jago, by Brown, and the college" (p. 67).

Of the three, only Chrystal got what he wanted because only
he was a heresthetician. Brown was good at helping people to
express the feelings they already had just beneath the surface
and built Jago's coalition in exactly this way. Chrystal, on the
other hand, tried to structure situations so that, willy-nilly,
something advantageous to him would perhaps occur. He was
just as opportunistic as Gouverneur Morris; like Morris, he

was driven by the desire to excel; but, just as Morris was idealistically devoted to the cause of a greater Union, so on a lesser scale Chrystal was devoted to an ideal of a flourishing college. Because he was this combination of the idealist and the heresthetician, in the end he had his way, both forcing the choice *and* getting the credit.

Chrystal's program, which meant far more to him than Jago, was to strengthen the college, and the subplot of the novel is his wooing of a benefactor. Brown had first scented the chance and called in Chrystal, who devoted "countless hours" to nurturing Sir Horace. Ultimately Sir Horace promised six fellowships, thereby increasing the size of the college by nearly half. This was the kind of thing Chrystal regarded as his real duty, and the election of a master was, if anything, a distraction.

At no time was Chrystal an intense partisan of Jago. Brown "drew him in" right away, but he never felt certain of Chrystal's allegiance. At least a half-dozen times throughout the novel, Brown suspected that Chrystal's interest was flagging, that he was slipping away, as indeed he was. Brown recognized, as Eliot perhaps did not, a difference in motivations. For Brown, the election of his friend Jago was an end in itself. For Chrystal it was only a means to a more innovative management of the college. So Brown was right to be constantly concerned with reinforcing Chrystal.

All this is made vividly clear at the receipt of Sir Horace's letter officially proposing his benefactions. Amid the general excitement and congratulations, Winslow, the Bursar, sits silent and shocked. As Bursar he should have been intimately involved in the long negotiations, but Chrystal and Brown have carefully kept him in ignorance because they feared his vicious tongue would put Sir Horace off. Toward the end of the meeting, Winslow resigns his office in shame. Jago comes to Winslow's defense, even though they are old enemies: "This is a wretched exchange . . . a fine Bursar for a rich man's charity" (p. 255). Eliot and Calvert admire Jago's "bravura," but Chrystal is not pleased. It takes the shine off his victory, and the next day he remarks rather petulantly to Brown that he can see the other side's case against Jago. "He's too much up and down," says Chrystal (p. 259); and perhaps, as Eliot surmises, that was when Chrystal's defection began.

Nevertheless, while Chrystal was in the coalition, he and he alone brought Jago within reach of victory. The college statutes required a clear majority of the fellows to elect, and, failing a majority, the choice reverted to the Visitor, a bishop otherwise unconnected with and uninterested in the college. Most fellows were deeply opposed to allowing the Visitor to appoint; yet the possibility was real. Jago and Crawford could not vote for themselves and would not vote for each other, so there were only eleven free votes from which a candidate needed seven for election. At a meeting Chrystal called to discuss the situation, he summarized the coalitions as they then were:

For Jago:	Brown
	Chrystal
	Eliot
	Calvert
	Luke
	and, possibly, Pilbrow, who, however, was abroad and might even not show up for the election.
For Crawford:	Despard-Smith
	Winslow
	Nightingale
	Getliffe
	and, possibly, Gay, whose forgetfulness rendered his allegiance doubtful.

Thus, the division was 5–4 among the confirmed adherents of one side or the other or, including doubtfuls, 6–5. Thus, neither side could elect because, as it stood, neither could get seven.

Chrystal then proposed his elegant maneuver. Let the others join him, he urged, in forcing the two candidates to vote for each other. They could, he said, if the candidates refused to comply, bring in an outsider rather than let the decision go to the Visitor. He managed to get three from each side to join in this threat and so, under duress, the candidates agreed. This maneuver, of course, gave Jago seven votes, at least on paper, and this was the closest he ever came to victory. It was a strong position, fashioned entirely by Chrystal; but Brown, ever suspicious, did not like it. " 'I'd rather,' he said, 'Chrystal was thinking more about getting Jago in than in keeping the Visitor out' " (p. 222). And Brown was right to be upset. It was Chrystal's heresthetic that brought Jago up, but Chrystal's motive was for himself to be in control and to make his control clear. That was what Brown feared.

Chrystal tried to carry off a similar coup after Jago's coalition declined from its high point. Pilbrow switched, then Gay reversed his vote, and the coalitions came to stand 5–5 or, counting Jago and Crawford, 6–6, with Gay's position uncertain. Chrystal called another meeting of which the purpose was clearly again to give Chrystal control. Again, Brown did not like it and was especially upset when Eliot reported that he and Calvert had almost certainly converted Gay, which, if true, would mean Jago still had seven votes. Chrystal refused to believe Eliot's report, perhaps because it eliminated the need for Chrystalization. So the meeting was held, but inconclusively. All night Chrystal tried to form a cave, offering a multitude of names from inside and outside the college to serve as an alternative to which both sides could rally. Chrystal even offered Brown, but not himself: "I'm not fit to be Master. Brown is. I'd serve under him and think myself lucky" (p. 316).

Chrystal couldn't break the apparent deadlock and so he chose the only remaining pathway to control. He spent the day before the election with Crawford and then changed his vote. As he told Brown, "I'm satisfied with Crawford . . . I've been with him all day. I've heard his views on the college. I like them. It's been a satisfactory day" (p. 335).

Thus, Chrystal made the move that brought Jago close to winning and also made the move that won for Crawford. Whatever happened, Chrystal forced the college into a position that, at the time, he wanted. He was not a superman, however. He failed, for example, to form a cave. Eliot wisely remarked, in just that connection: "in all the moves of politics, dexterity is meaningless, even will itself does not avail, unless there is some spot in one's opponent ready to be convinced" (p. 313). Heresthetic is neither rhetoric nor magic. The heresthetician can neither create preferences nor hypnotize. What he can do is probe until he finds some new alternative, some new dimension, that strikes a spark in the preference of others. Sometimes he fails, as in Chrystal's cave; sometimes he succeeds, as when Chrystal raised the dimension of choice by the Visitor. And when all else fails, he has his own vote to manipulate, just as Chrystal did.

One should remember, I believe, just what skillful heresthetician can do. Engage their attention, draw them into the struggle, and no future is certain. Poor Jago. Naively he believed that victory was his and prematurely revealed his ambition and pride. Thus he was rendered vulnerable to the natural forces around him. Chrystal's heresthetic raised him up and then cast him down. That is something to remember.

Novels are complex matters, not quite as complex as life itself, but just as complex as history. Some readers may believe that I have selected just one strand out of the complexity of *The Masters*. Of course, I have selected just one strand, but I believe it is the most important. In his brief preface, Snow commented on what in the novel is fictional and what is real. He said his people were "from many sources" and there was no "actual election" like his imaginary one. Still, he added, "there is a tradition of a last-minute change of fortune early in the century, and a well authenticated one in Mark Pattison's *Memoirs*" (p. vii). All this suggests that Snow himself thought that the switch was the central theme, especially since there is little similarity between Jago's and Pattison's cases except the fact of the switch. (In 1851, going into the election for the Rectorship of Lincoln College, Oxford, Pattison had a five to four majority. There was a defection to the candidate of the other side, one Kay; so Pattison lost, but at least his party found an alternative on Kay's side in one Thompson, whom Pattison's party then elected with their four votes and Thompson's. Not at all the same kind of story, except in the switch itself.)

More to the point, however, two pages from the end of the novel, when the votes are read out, the reader discovers that Chrystal's Christian names are Charles Percy, exactly like C. P. Snow. Is this Chrystal of Snow a facet that reveals himself, reflecting his decision and his concerns?

6 CAMOUFLAGING THE GERRYMANDER

One heresthetical maneuver already described is that of raising against a disputed alternative still another dimension of judgment that splits the opposition. This is, for example, what Lincoln (and indeed the whole Whig-Republican succession) did by raising the issue of slavery to complicate the dispute between agrarian and commercial expansionists. This is also what Chauncey DePew did by proposing a force bill to complicate the dispute over the direct election of senators. This is what Chrystal did when he used the threat of selection by the Visitor to force Jago and Crawford to vote for each other. For the convenience of a name, I will call this heresthetical device *increasing dimensionality*.

As should be expected there is a converse maneuver, *fixing dimensionality*. When the currently winning side anticipates that the opposition will add a dimension to split the winners, it is open to herestheticians of the majority to block the anticipated addition. This is what I will call Fixing Dimensionality and I will describe it in this essay.

Once upon a time there was a city manager who was uncommonly astute. She anticipated, perhaps correctly, that the Democratic majority on the city council would lose the next election. Since she had been hired by and faithfully served Democrats, she anticipated also, and for certain correctly, that if the Republicans won they would fire her. So she undertook to protect herself by, among other things, a brilliant application of Fixing Dimensionality in an act of camouflage.

As this story begins, partisan control of the city council was very much in doubt. Republicans had had a majority during most of the previous hundred years, barring only a few rare accidents that permitted Democratic control. Nevertheless, the Democrats were now very much on the upswing by reason of the movement of population in and out of the city (Republican voters out, Democratic voters in) and by reason of a generational change in the partisan identification of several ethnic groups (e.g., from Republican families, young blacks and Italians turning Democratic). Five years prior to this story, the upswing had produced Democratic control of the council, and twice the party retained control with narrow victories and a five to four margin. Dissatisfaction, of course, accumulates in five years, especially when the governing coalition is minimal. So the Democrats had good reason to surmise that, even though demography and time were on their side, they might easily lose this election. In fact, as it turned out, they were wrong. Because of their worry, they put all their energy, resources, and intelligence into the campaign. This investment probably saved the day, or so it seems, because two years later in similar circumstances they lost. This later election was in many ways a rerun of the first. The Democrats still had only narrow control and they still faced a lot of dissatisfaction. But they were not quite so worried because, after all, they had won in similar circumstances two years previously. So perhaps they did not worry and work as hard in the later election and they lost, which suggests that it was work and worry that saved the day in the election of this story. Nevertheless, six years after this election they regained control a second time, and they have retained it ever since. Nowadays the Republicans are never able to win more than one seat out of nine and the Democrats seem to be as surely and certainly in control as Republicans had been in an earlier era.

The event occurred, then, exactly in the center of the twelve-year long transition from Republican to Democratic hegemony. Consequently, when the participants in this event appear uncertain about partisan strength, we can, with the historian's advantage, be sure they were justified in their uncertainty.

The city manager was, however, a creative woman and she figured out an expedient maneuver—namely, to gerrymander—

that is, to rearrange the boundaries of districts so that with the same number of votes the Democrats could win another seat. This is a well-tested political device, increasingly popular in recent years because of encouragement from the Supreme Court, though the name goes back to Elbridge Gerry and a Massachusetts election early in the nineteenth century. Gerrymandering politicians usually gain from it, but still it has one possibly serious drawback: many citizens think of it, at least in the abstract, as cheating. Hence, the Outs can accuse the Ins of ruthless unfairness in one thing and perhaps, by inference, in many things. By this addition of a procedural issue to all the substantive issues, the Outs may heresthetically regain all, and more, that the Ins have obtained by the gerrymander itself. So gerrymanders are best done surreptitiously—as when redistricting is undertaken in response to a new census—though it is hard to keep quiet about a maneuver that by its very nature must be public.

In this particular case it was more difficult than usual to gerrymander without being noticed because the Democrats had redistricted just as soon as they gained control of the council five years previously. They believed that some of the districts were rotten boroughs. And they were right. The boundaries had not been revised for thirty years and the population changes in that time had greatly swelled one Democratic district and emptied a Republican one. Not unjustifiably, the Democrats believed this population drift—or silent gerrymander, as it is often called—had enabled Republicans to win an extra seat. So the Democrats redistricted, forcing a Republican to retire and perhaps thereby gaining a seat. In that earlier redistricting, the Democrats had not, in my opinion, gerrymandered in the sense that they drew the boundaries to get more seats than their share of the popular vote. Incumbents must, of course, draw boundaries, and they should be expected to draw advantageously for themselves, but this can hardly be called unfair if it does not give them more seats than their total vote justifies.

Now, however, in her position of extreme danger, the city manager thought a gerrymander seemed possible—a completion, in a sense, of the earlier redistricting. Surely it would be advantageous. Still, it was three more years to the next census. There was no conventional rationale for taking up the matter of boundaries. So, if the council were to redistrict, the accusation of cheating would inevitably follow. In spite of all this, the manager invented a way to gerrymander and to camouflage it. So—the Democrats squeaked through to victory and she held on to her job for two more years.

The election system within which the manager had to work was structured thus: the council had nine members, five elected at large and four elected in districts. The terms of members were four years and the two categories were chosen at alternate biennial elections. Coming up, of course, was a district year, while the at-large members elected the previous year would hold over. The city, which had grown up around a crossroads, was roughly circular in shape. The boundaries of the districts followed just about the original crossroads and divided the districts into the four quarters of a circle. The partisan division of the council was:

	Democrat	Republican	Total
At Large	3	2	5
District	2	2	4
Total	5	4	9

The parties were, of course, divided about equally in seats and in voters in the whole city. One might expect, therefore, that in the next election the outcome would, as before, be a two-to-two split. But the manager had purchased polling research and was fairly certain that in one of the two current Democratic districts the outcome would be unfavorable. (The Democratic incumbent had won this district in the last election by something of a fluke, by reason, that is, of the retirement of the Republican councilman and a consequent split in the Republican party. That split was now healed and Republicans might reasonably be expected to regain the district.) Thus, even though the Democrats had, perhaps, a small majority, the prospective election results were:

District	Current Member		Proportion of City Voters		Prospective Outcome	
	Dem.	Rep.	Dem.	Rep.	Dem.	Rep.
Northeast	x		20	5	x	
Southeast	x		10	15		x
Southwest		x	11	14		x
Northwest		x	12	13		x
Totals	2	- 2	53	- 47	1	- 3

So, with the holdover members at large, the partisan division would be: 4 Democrats and 5 Republicans.

Of course, this might be prevented by redistricting. For example, in the two eastern districts taken together, the Democrats had an advantage of 3 to 2; but, in two districts taken separately, they had a 4 to 1 advantage in one and a 2 to 3 disadvantage in the other. By transferring areas between the two, each district might be made to mirror the 3 to 2 Democratic advantage on the east side. The city manager had, in fact, worked out a redistricting plan, much more complicated, of course, than my example and involving transfers among all four districts. Her plan did seem to guarantee Democratic victories in both the eastern districts. Naturally, she was eager to have the council enact it.

There were at least two difficulties. One, already mentioned, was the danger of creating an issue of Democratic ruthlessness. This danger was doubled by the fact that there had already been one redistricting during the decade, and a premature second one would indeed appear self-serving. The second difficulty was that the redistricting, while clearly to the manager's advantage, was not clearly to the advantage of the Democratic council members. Both these difficulties might lead the council to refuse to enact the manager's plan. But fortunately for her, these superficially different difficulties had the same solution, so that the council did in fact redistrict.

The second difficulty was quite real. There were three possible outcomes for the Democrats:

1. A clear majority: if they gerrymandered and succeeded they would end up with *five,* even perhaps *six,* council seats;
2. A maximal minority: if they did not gerrymander, they would, if the survey research was correct, end up with *four* seats;
3. A minimal minority: if they gerrymandered and failed, they might win no districts and end up with only the *three* at-large seats.

From the point of view of the city manager, only the first outcome was desirable. The second and third, under either of which she would lose her job, had about the same value for her, namely zero. From the point of view of the council members, however, four seats were significantly better than three. Consider the situation of the council member in the northeast district, the currently safe incumbent. A failed gerrymander would mean the defeat of two incumbents including himself, while no gerrymander at all would mean that he would at least survive. Naturally, the northeast member would, by a wide margin, prefer no gerrymander to a failed gerrymander. On the other hand, the southeast member, very likely to lose without a gerrymander, would probably prefer even a failed gerrymander, which would give him some chance, to no gerrymander at all. Between these two opposing interests, there might well have been a stand-off. Throwing the manager's interest into the balance may have outweighed the interest of the safe incumbent and of course he might be bought off with the promise of patronage—at the state level, say—if the gerrymander failed. Still, the other Democratic members had an interest also. Under state law, two-thirds of a council was necessary to issue bonds for capital improvements. Hence a minority larger than one-third could trade its approval of bonds for all manner of other political concessions. Since the Republican minority was currently bargaining in just this way, all the Democratic council members must have been aware of the possibility. The four Democratic members who would survive even without a gerrymander must have therefore placed some positive value on outcome (2), that is, a maximal minority with no gerrymander at all.

In choosing between the two alternatives, the council Democrats as a group had to balance the values of the alternatives in light of the uncertainties:

(a) The value from gerrymandering: If the decision is to gerrymander, either outcome (1) or outcome (3) may result. Hence, the value of gerrymandering is a mixture of the best and the worst. This, then, is the chance of getting the value of outcome (1) plus the chance of getting the value of outcome (3). Since, presumably, the value of outcome (3) is zero for everyone, this calculation reduces to the chance of getting the best outcome—(1)—times the value of that outcome.

(b) The value from not gerrymandering: This is exactly the value from outcome (2).

If a council member judges the chance of a failed gerrymander to be very great, then the chance of getting outcome (1) is fairly low and the gerrymander itself is not worth much. Perhaps it is even worth less than not gerrymandering. In this circumstance, reasonable men might hotly dispute the choice of tactics.

Nevertheless, the council Democrats did choose to gerrymander, which is excellent evidence that they believed the chance of failure was small. Given the danger of Republicans raising and exploiting the charge of ruthlessness, this is a surprising belief. What led the Democrats to hold it?

The usual explanation of why gerrymandering politicians are not worried by the charge of ruthlessness is that they do not believe voters will be influenced by it. Voters of the other party will of course resent the gerrymander; but, since they would not vote for the gerrymanderers anyway, their resentment is ineffectual. As for supporters of the gerrymandering party, they, by definition, want the policies of their party carried out and the gerrymander increases the chance of this happening. That these voters would punish their own leaders for successful ruthlessness is improbable at best. Hence the only voters likely to respond favorably to the charge of ruthlessness are those practically indifferent to both parties. Presumably there are very few in this last category. Nevertheless, the charge of ruthlessness may have some heresthetical effect when either (a) the margin between the parties is very tight, so that a small number of switchers makes a difference; or (b) the ruthlessness is particularly flagrant so that more voters than usual are motivated to place "decency" above partisan success. In this council election, the margin was indeed small and the gerrymander promised to be especially visible. So the chance was not negligible that the gerrymander might fail by reason of the issue of ruthlessness. How, then, could the council members have been persuaded that the danger of failure was remote?

The answer is camouflage. It is no mean accomplishment to camouflage the second redistricting in five years without even the apparent justification of shifts of population. How did the manager do it? The answer is she used *Baker v. Carr* and *Reynolds v. Sims.*

During the rapid and extreme urbanization in the first half of this century, many state legislators from small towns were reluctant to redistrict. Doing so tended to unseat their old friends and many of themselves, replacing them with unknown urban politicians. Some states were scandalous. Tennessee did not redistrict from 1901 until judicially forced to in the mid-1960s. Illinois and several others did not redistrict after 1911. In some states the disparity between the largest and smallest districts exceeded a factor of ten (e.g., Harris County, Texas, with Houston, eventually had over a million people, while Sam Rayburn's district north of Dallas had well under a hundred thousand—that Sam Rayburn's district was favored explains a lot about the motivation). Many lawsuits had been brought, petitioning courts to take a hand in the process, but for a long time the Supreme Court refused to interfere in what it described as "political" matters. Finally, however, in the cases of *Baker v. Carr* (1962) and *Reynolds v. Sims* (1964), the Court did order equalization of the size of districts both for Congress and for all state legislative bodies. During the mid-

1960s, therefore, a huge number of lawsuits were brought to force all sorts of bodies, including city councils, to redistrict themselves equally.

The city council of our story had in fact done so in the Democrats' first redistricting, which followed just after *Baker v. Carr*. Still, the largest and smallest districts varied by over 10 percent. And that fact was the city manager's opportunity.

She persuaded the Democrats on the council to agree to the following scenario:

> Stage 1:The city manager would arrange for a nonpolitical friend to sue the city council in the federal court, claiming that the 10 percent differential violated his civil rights and denied him the equal protection of the laws.

> Stage 2:At the next council meeting after the filing of the suit, the Democrats would introduce an ordinance embodying the manager's plan for the districts. They would explain that they did so, first, out of simple justice and, second, because it was wastefully expensive to defend themselves against a lawsuit that, since they were in the wrong, they were sure to lose.

> Stage 3:Then, finally, at the next following council meeting, they would enact the ordinance.

The manager claimed that, in several ways, this procedure would divert criticism. First off, she argued, the redistricting would appear to the public to respond to external legal pressures and have nothing to do with a gerrymander. Widespread public knowledge, as then existed, of the issues involved in redistricting lawsuits would add credibility to that appearance. Republicans probably would be unable, therefore, to level the accusation of unfairness. The Democrats, instead of appearing to cheat, would appear to be promptly and meritoriously repairing an obvious defect in the existing ordinance.

In the second place, she argued, a suit in the federal court, as was jurisdictionally appropriate given the allegations, precluded a Republican lawsuit in the county court (i.e., in the state court system). This was no small advantage. The federal judge was a Democrat. All the county judges were Republicans. A Democratic lawsuit in the federal court would presumably get preferential treatment, and the federal judge certainly would not allow county judges to interfere with a partisan matter before him. If the Democrats were to gerrymander without first placing the matter in the federal court, Republican council members would be certain to sue in some state court. With judicial help, they could tie up the gerrymander in procedural knots until the deadline had passed for enactment for the next election. With the case in the federal court, untouchable by Republican maneuvers, the Democrats could rush through stage 3 of the scenario before there was much public discussion and before the Republicans could raise the issue of fairness.

Of course, as the manager pointed out, the Republican minority and the journalists on the city hall beat would see through the scenario. But still, no one would be able to cry "foul" because, unquestionably, the lawsuit was entirely appropriate under the doctrine of *Reynolds v. Sims* and the nonpolitical friend could hardly be accused of participating in a gerrymander.

The whole thing, the manager promised, would be over in two weeks: one week for the filing of the suit and the introduction of the ordinance, another week for passing the ordinance. The word *gerrymander* would probably never be uttered in public. The issue of fairness and ruthlessness would never be raised. And by election time the following fall, hardly anybody would remember the redistricting, except, perhaps, the council members themselves.

This scenario and argument were persuasive to the Democrats on the council, even the one with the ultra safe district. So they enacted the manager's redistricting plan.

The manager was, as it turned out, almost exactly correct in predicting the course of events. The scenario played out swiftly, in two weeks, as promised. Republicans fumed, but in private. Journalists poked and sniffed, trying to find an angle on which to hang the story of the gerrymander. But they could find none, for everything was meretriciously smothered in the doctrine of *Baker v. Carr* and *Reynolds v. Sims*. The word *gerrymander* did appear once in a newspaper, but that was in

the column of a journalist so ill-tempered and caustic that he
influenced very few people. Even he could not break through
the hypocrisy of the Democrats' ostentatious public claims of
obedience to the law.

So the gerrymander was carried through surreptitiously, as
all good gerrymanders should be. The Democrats kept their
majority and the manager her job. This was an appropriate
outcome because, however much some may condemn the
manager's heresthetic, extraordinary cleverness deserves some
reward.

It has been traditional in our popular public morality to
condemn gerrymanders. I have read much on this subject and
can recall no defense except the childish excuse that everyone
else does it. Yet it is certainly true that politicians of all parties
gerrymander frequently, especially since the Supreme Court
required regular redistricting in the cases elaborating on *Baker
v. Carr.*

Furthermore, the Court both condoned and encouraged gerrymanders by two doctrines. First, the judicial enforcement of
exact equality in the population of districts requires that legislators work out in detail plans for the assignment of territory
down to the precinct level. It would be morally asking too
much of any group of people, I believe, to require that they
assign territory in a way disadvantageous to themselves. So we
do not require or expect this. Nor can we ask them to be
exactly fair. By reason of irreconcilable conflicts among several standards of fairness, it is technically impossible to be
exactly fair, an impossibility that has been neatly demonstrated by Richard Niemi and John Deegan in "A Theory of
Political Districting," *American Political Science Review* 72
(December, 1978): 1304–23. So, by default, politicians must
gerrymander if they redistrict, and redistrict they must by di-
rective of the Court. Evidently the judges have decided that,
between rotten boroughs and gerrymanders, gerrymanders are
the lesser sin.

The second judicial doctrine encouraging gerrymanders is
the requirement that blacks be put in districts in such a way as

to enable them to elect black representatives. This is, of course, classic gerrymandering. It is defended and justified as a kind of affirmative action. But all gerrymanders everywhere are defended and justified as helping out some worthy people. It is hard to distinguish the present Court's good cause from, say, the cause of Elbridge Gerry and the Massachusetts Democracy in 1811. So, in this respect, the Court has consciously condoned, approved, and encouraged gerrymandering in general. What can be said about popular notions of unfairness, cheating, and ruthless self-serving when the keeper of the national collective conscience tells us that gerrymanders are a good thing?

Given this conflict between judges' taste and popular morality, my inclination is to say, on the judges' side, that gerrymandering is both inevitable and not preventable, but, on the popular side, that it still should not go too far. In the end, a party ought to get, I believe, (very) roughly the number of seats that its total vote justifies. If it does not, year after year, then something manifestly unfair is going on.

The Democrats in this story did not do excessively well, though they doubtless gained the incumbents' advantage. In this sense, their gerrymander is unexceptionable.

Thus, given that they did nothing improper in the ordinance itself, it seems to me that the way they presented it to the public was their own business. Surely they were not required to present it in a way that would enable the Republican her-estheticians to defeat them with an additional dimension. So those readers who have, as they followed my story, condemned the city manager and her cohorts, I beg to reexamine their judgment. Probably, like me, they will on reflection conclude that her action was innocuous and her heresthetic brilliant.

7 PLINY THE YOUNGER ON PARLIAMENTARY LAW

In a legislative body the agenda is controlled, for the most part, by the official leaders. But ordinary members do have defenses against leaders' domination. One defense is the introduction of divisive amendments, really a kind of agenda control by back-benchers, as practiced, for example, by Chauncey DePew. Another defense is strategic voting, which is voting contrary to one's immediate tastes in order to obtain an advantage in the long run. Sometimes, as in the story I am about to relate, leaders and ordinary members compete, the one manipulating the agenda, the other countering with strategic voting. In this instance, the ordinary members neutralized the leader, although against less acute opposition the leader might have come out ahead.

This story is particularly impressive to me because it shows that heresthetics is an ancient art, practiced skillfully in the Roman Senate about 100 A.D., probably during the reign of the Emperor Trajan. Heresthetical maneuvers were rarely described by ancient writers, except for Thucydides. But we do have at least one other detailed account in the letters of the younger Pliny. A tale such as this is a valuable reminder that the art of heresthetics is not just a feature of the complications of modern civil life, but is, rather, a universal practice of mankind. Wherever people make decisions in groups, it is possible to practice heresthetics. If we had inherited enough historical detail, I suspect we would find tales similar to this one in the annals of the advisers of the Pharaohs and the Incas.

The younger Pliny was a Roman barrister who made a career of the practice of chancery law and of various prosecutorial, judicial, and fiscal magistracies. At the end of his life, he was a troubleshooter in Asia Minor for the Emperor Trajan. On the civilian side of things, this was a fairly typical career for the several hundred senators who, at any one time, managed the Roman Empire. But Pliny differed from most others because he also had literary ambitions. This was perhaps a family trait: his uncle, the elder Pliny, though by profession a soldier and a governor, also wrote voluminously as an avocation. But the elder Pliny is now remembered mainly for his natural history, while the younger Pliny invented a new art form, the familiar letter. Since he himself collected his letters for publication, they never delve far beneath the public surface, either psychologically or socially. Still they give us, with his permission and in the way he wished it, a glimpse into the family, literary, and professional life of a genial, humane, and somewhat self-satisfied Roman gentleman.

The letters deal with many topics: his writings, houses, and farms; his family, colleagues, friends, sponsors, and protégés; and gossip, prodigies, and so on. One topic that often recurs comprises cases from his professional life. He used the letters, so it seems, to justify actions that others had perhaps criticized—a surefire way to have the last word. Thanks to this literary style, we have a wealth of concrete details about a few of his actions, one of which occurred in the course of his parliamentary manipulation.

As presiding officer, he ruled—unsuccessfully—that the Senate use a procedure that would lead to an outcome he desired; but his ruling must have seemed unfair to many senators. So his letter (book 8, letter 14) about this event is in fact an elaborate justification of his ruling, although it is couched in the form of a request for advice on precedents from Titius Aristo, whom he addresses as his friend and as an authority on parliamentary law. In several generations of imperial rule, senators had forgotten customary procedure, so Pliny said, and the letter is thus a request for precedent. Actually, however, it is his argument for the procedure he used, regardless of what may or may not have been the customary rule. Indeed, Pliny tells Titius that, although the case is now closed, he is going to explain his arguments in his own way without the interruptions he had to put up with in the Senate.

The case arose when the consul Afranius Dexter was found dead. He might have been a suicide or he might have been killed by his servants; and if he was killed by his servants, they might have done so either with criminal intent or at his request. Consequently, his freedmen were on trial before the Senate. (Pliny tells us nothing about the household slaves beyond implying that their fate had been decided previously. The commentators tell us that, in such cases, typically the slaves were executed wholesale, and Pliny perhaps implies that that happened in this case. Roman aristocrats took no chances with slave revolts.)

Concerning the fate of the freedmen, there were three opinions or, in a sense, three parties:

1. For acquittal, A. (Presumably these people believed Afranius was a coward who was unable to commit suicide and who had therefore instructed his servants to kill him. Incidentally, Pliny describes braver men who killed themselves when old and sick, a reasonable action in an era without painkillers. Unlike the cowardly Afranius, these other suicides, including, perhaps, Titius Aristo himself, thoughtfully and decently avoided involving their households in the act. The most politically self-conscious of the suicides was one Cornelius Rufus, gouty in all limbs, who nevertheless waited to starve himself to death until he had outlived the tyrant Domitian.)

2. For banishment, B. (Perhaps these people believed that Afranius had indeed ordered his own murder but nevertheless wished to impose some punishment because then, as now, it was against the law to assist a suicide.)

3. For condemnation to death, C. (Doubtless these people suffered from the "we'll-all-be-murdered-in-our-beds" syndrome.)

The first group, which, it is important to note, included Pliny himself, was the largest, but no group was a majority in itself. Any two groups together could have won. This suggests a ratio something like 45:35:20, where the party for acquittal has 45 percent and the party for banishment 35.

It is easy to reconstruct the full preference orderings for two of the groups. Pliny tells us that banishment is closer to acquittal than to death. Hence the group for acquittal must have ordered thus:

> (1) A (acquittal), B (banishment), C (condemnation to death).

Pliny also tells us that those who voted for execution and banishment ultimately sat together on the initiative of the mover of the motion for death. Hence the group for condemnation to death must have ordered:

> (3) C (condemnation to death), B (banishment), A (acquittal).

The ordering for the group for banishment is not quite so clear. Certainly, banishment is in the first place; but does death or acquittal come second? Pliny's judgments confuse us: If banishment is closer to acquittal than to death, then acquittal should be second. But if those for banishment and execution sat together, then execution should be second. However, if, as Pliny hints, the decision to sit together was made unilaterally by the leader of the party for execution, then the seating arrangements imply nothing about the second choice. So, given Pliny's other remark that banishment is closer to acquittal than to death, the group for banishment must have ordered:

> (2) B (banishment), A (acquittal), C (condemnation to death).

And, to summarize, the groups were:

1. Acquitters: ABC—45%
2. Banishers: BAC—35%
3. Executioners: CBA—20%

As presiding officer, Pliny was uncertain, or professed to be, about how to put the question. We can compare his choice of procedure with modern criminal procedure, even though it may be no better or worse than his. Today a court would first decide whether the accused was guilty or innocent. If innocent, acquittal would end the matter. If guilty, the court would then decide on the punishment, banishment or death. Using this modern procedure, at the first question those for death and banishment would join in voting guilty, which would thus win with 55 percent of the ballots. Then, on the choice between banishment and death, those for acquittal and banishment would join in voting for banishment, which would win with 75 percent.

This modern procedure is "binary" in the sense that it pits a pair of alternatives against each other, with the survivor either being the ultimate winner or being pitted against another alternative. Given the distribution of tastes in Pliny's Senate, any binary procedure would lead to banishment as the outcome. This is owing to the fact that banishment is a "Condorcet winner"—that is, it has a clear majority over each of the other alternatives. Of course, a Condorcet winner need not exist (A might beat B, B beat C, and C beat A), but if a Condorcet winner does exist, a binary procedure will reveal it.

This feature is what renders binary procedures morally attractive to moderns. Morally speaking, one wants to have confidence that voting truly and fairly amalgamates the variety of voters' tastes into a unique social choice. Surely one has the most such confidence when an absolute majority places one alternative first in their orders of preference. Unfortunately,

FIGURE 1
Modern Procedure

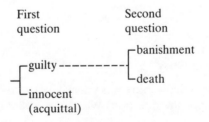

First question   Second question

guilty ——————— banishment / death

innocent (acquittal)

when, as in the case of Afranius Dexter's freedmen, there are more than two alternatives, often no alternative has a majority of first places. So one needs a definition of winning that is both easier to satisfy and yet still fair. And a good second best is the Condorcet criterion: the winner is that alternative which has a majority over each of the others. The moral justification of binary procedures is, then, that they satisfy the second-best or Condorcet criterion, if it can be satisfied at all.

I emphasize our modern preference for binary procedures because Pliny self-interestedly and self-righteously rejected a binary procedure in this case. He chose instead to put the question in what might be called a ternary form (see figure 2). That is, he required that each of the three senators who had moved a motion sit in separate places, intending to choose as the winner that alternative whose mover had the most voters sitting near him. This procedure, of course, utilizes the plurality criterion which is quite different from the Condorcet criterion. The plurality winner is that alternative which has the most first-place votes, and need not be the same as the Condorcet winner. Indeed, in this case, the plurality winner is A, acquittal, with perhaps 45 percent of the votes, but A loses to the Condorcet winner, B, or banishment, in a head-to-head contest, 45 percent for acquittal and 55 percent for banishment.

It is easy enough to see why Pliny wanted to use a ternary procedure. He himself favored acquittal, which would lose by any binary procedure and, presumably, win by his ternary procedure. So he exercised his power as presiding officer to force the adoption of his own first choice. As he tells us, however, his explanation of his ruling was interrupted—one can imagine a scene of considerable tumult and shouting—and

FIGURE 2
Pliny's Procedure

```
                         ┌─ acquittal
        ─────────────────┼─ banishment
                         └─ death
```

this suggests that the senators knew very well what he was doing and that his ruling violated their sense of fair play.

And well it might. Pliny tells us enough about Roman parliamentary forms to indicate that the then ancient formula for taking a division was binary. It began with "All who agree go to this side," which is clearly binary. It continued, so he said, in what appears to be an n-ary form: "all who support any other proposal go to the side you support." Pliny interprets this as implying n sides (or, in this case, three), which supports his case. But n sides seems wholly implausible and, given the binary tone of the first part of the formula, one suspects that the intention of the latter part was binary also. Clearly, from the described interruptions, many senators thought so too. Pliny's ruling must have seemed quite arbitrary and unfair, especially since the commentators tell us that it was customary to vote on banishment and death separately and in succession, and this is substantially a binary procedure, which in this case would, of course, have resulted in banishment (see figure 3).

Pliny had his way, however, about the form of the question. So long as the motions for death and banishment were both before the Senate, he forced the supporters of each to sit apart. He was about to win.

But the mover of the motion for the death sentence and the leader of executioners was just as acute a parliamentarian as Pliny. Putting the best face on his defeat, Pliny tells us that the mover of the motion for death was "convinced" by Pliny's arguments. So he (i.e., the mover) dropped his motion and crossed the floor to sit with the supporters of banishment. His

FIGURE 3
Traditional Roman Procedure

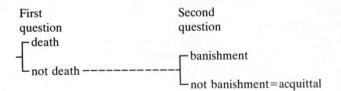

supporters followed him and so banishment won. Pliny lost, despite his (perhaps too clever) parliamentary maneuver.

Pliny's maneuver depended for its success on each senator voting myopically—that is, voting for the first alternative in his preference order, regardless of consequences. If the senators had acted as he expected, the supporters of banishment and of death would not have combined forces, thus assuring victory for acquittal. But the laws of nature do not require that men behave foolishly. We can consider the consequences of alternative actions and choose the one that seems likely to turn out best. In the case of voting, this means to vote strategically, that is, to vote to obtain the best possible outcome, not merely to express an opinion. Strategic voting in this situation required the supporters of the death sentence to vote for their second-place alternative in order to prevent the victory of their third-place alternative, which is, of course, precisely what the senators did. They may have been illiberal, but they were not stupid.

In general, parliamentary situations are like this. Leaders have the kind of procedural power that Pliny exercised, but back-benchers can counter with strategic voting. So the fox can be outfoxed. And thus a balance can be maintained, often resulting, as here, in the selection of the Condorcet winner, which is a socially better outcome, I believe, than the plurality winner that would have been selected by Pliny's procedure.

In reflecting upon Pliny's letter, perhaps the most remarkable feature is not the story itself, but Pliny's defense of his action. He claimed that everybody on the same side ought to have the same structure of preferences—so, for example, three structures should represent three sides. Some modern commentators (as well, presumably, as the opposing senators) have interpreted his argument as simply an unsuccessful attempt to pull the wool over the senators' eyes. But an alternative explanation is just as feasible, namely, that Pliny genuinely misunderstood the nature of voting. In the first explanation, Pliny is not only a conscious schemer trying to push the Senate where a majority will not go, but also a conscious

dissembler whose justification of his ruling is merely ideological dressing for what he recognized, otherwise, as his naked
self-interest. In the second explanation, which I must say ap-
peals to me, Pliny is assumed to speak ignorantly but innocently. Of course, his ruling did blatantly express his own
preference. But he may very well have been confused about
the meaning of voting and majorities. If so, then his self-
defense was at least honest. He remains a schemer, of
course, just like most other men, but he is not omniscient.
That he took a wrong position because it was to his advantage is clear, and this renders him culpable on a practical
level. But he seems not to have had the slightest suspicion of
how wrong his position was, which absolves him of culpability
on an intellectual level.

The reason I am inclined to take this second, more lenient
view of Pliny's letter is that still today a similar confusion
echoes in classrooms and forums. If, after centuries of practice, we still, often innocently, make the same mistakes as
Pliny, then we can hardly call him a liar and an ideologist. But
we can learn from his mistake.

Pliny's fundamental error was his belief that everyone on the
same side has (or ought to have) the same opinions. This was
historically untrue in the very case he analyzed. The ultimate
senatorial majority was composed of banishers (with BAC)
and executioners (with CBA). Of the three pairs of alternatives (A against B, B against C, A against C), the two groups
in the majority agree only in preferring B to A. Otherwise, the
banishers like A better than C while the executioners like C
better than A. Similarly, the banishers like B better than C,
while the executioners are opposite. The actual winning majority thus disagreed on the ordering of two out of the three
pairs. Clearly, majorities do not in fact always share the same
opinions.

This fact disturbed Pliny, and his main argument in favor of
his ternary procedure was that it forced the supporters of each
motion to have homogeneous opinions. Should Pliny have
been disturbed, as he said he was, by the fact that banishers
and executioners might vote together on one issue (guilty or

innocent) and then oppose each other on another issue (punishment)? To most modern parliamentarians, Pliny's uneasiness betrays a misunderstanding of what we—I mean both we professional parliamentarians and we professional students of social choice—now believe to be the essence of voting. We recognize that opinions are as various as fingerprints and so we expect majorities on one motion to consist of opponents on an immediately previous motion. We agree with the aphorism that politics, or in this case voting, makes strange bedfellows. What Pliny found disturbing, we believe to be normal.

But, of course, our difference in belief does not make either him or us right. Perhaps we can understand the deeper moral implications of the difference if we examine what it generally implies about moral standards for voting. Pliny clearly placed great emphasis on coherence. A majority either ought to make sense philosophically, he argued, or it ought not to be brought into existence by a head count. We, on the other hand, ask less of a majority. We recognize that its coherence can be obtained only at the cost of concentrating power in an autocrat or in oligarchs to police the views of its members. (This proposition is indeed the essence of Arrow's Theorem, though as a practical point it was understood by James Madison two hundred years ago.) We therefore reject the idea of a boss and opt for the autonomy of the individual voter. Furthermore, we interpret majorities as no more than artifacts of the head count, and we specifically deny that they make sense independently of the arithmetic. We see in Pliny's emphasis on coherence the roots of majority tyranny against which we have erected constitutional barriers such as the separation of powers. So there really is something at stake morally in this dispute. What started as an apparently simple matter of parliamentary law turns out to involve contrasting views about individual autonomy and, even more, about the appropriate instruments to preserve political liberty.

I think it likely that, with deeper thought, Pliny would have joined our side. He was, as his position on the issue in this case reveals, a liberal and humane man. Had he recognized that his action and his argument placed coherence above autonomy and justified demagoguery, I suspect that he would have reversed himself. I do not mean that he would not have tried to manipulate the Senate. As a reasonable man, he might very well—perhaps should—have done that. But at least he would not have tried to clothe his manipulation in a morally dubious theory.

Sources: Pliny's letter was brought to the attention of social choice theorists by Robin Farquharson, who used it as the running example in his *Theory of Voting* (New Haven: Yale University Press, 1969; accepted as a dissertation at Oxford in 1957). Unfortunately, Farquharson had available to him only an eighteenth-century translation by a translator who did not seem to understand the parliamentary issues involved and therefore did not see what happened at the end of the event. In 1963, however, Betty Radice published *The Letters of the Younger Pliny* (Harmondsworth: Penguin Books, 1963), which contains a sensitive and perceptive translation of letter 14 of book 8. I was much helped in understanding Pliny's letter and Radice's translation by my late colleague and superb Latinist, Maurice C. Cunningham. An exhaustive recent commentary, A. N. Sherwin-White, *The Letters of Pliny: A Historical and Social Commentary* (Oxford: Clarendon Press, 1966) exists, but it does not shed much light on this letter because, unlike Farquharson and Radice, Sherwin-White does not seem to understand the parliamentary situation in which Pliny found himself.

8 TRADING VOTES AT
THE CONSTITUTIONAL CONVENTION

In the public imagination legislators are constantly trading votes. Just as in the case of describing other popular but slightly disreputable activities like drinking alcohol, we have coined a variety of synonyms for vote-trading, such as "log-rolling," "back-scratching," or "going along," as in the practical cynicism of Sam Rayburn's remark "To get along, go along." The proliferation of synonyms reveals our (possibly naive) belief in the universality as well as the mild vulgarity of trading votes. It is even possible, as it happens, to date our sensitivity to the practice. In the latter quarter of the nineteenth century, at least seven states prohibited vote-trading by constitution or statute. No one, so far as I know, was ever prosecuted, and surely the practice has not abated since then.

Vote-trading is indeed an important heresthetic device. In manipulating political situations to one's advantage, it is not always possible to engage in grand maneuvers like increasing or fixing dimensionality. But one can always advantageously manage parliamentary situations, either by exploiting the rules, which is what presiding officers and agenda committees can do, or by casting one's own vote strategically, which is what ordinary members can do. Pliny's opponents cast their votes strategically for banishment instead of condemnation to death, an action they could undertake entirely on their own. Sometimes, however, strategic voting requires the cooperation of an erstwhile opponent with whom one trades votes for mutual advantage.

Widespread as vote-trading is thought to be, it is difficult to find well-documented and admitted instances of it. For one reason, politicians do not like to talk about it. When they do so, they reveal both that they have bought another's vote and that they have, for instrumental reasons, voted contrary to what they truly believe. That is, the vote-traders, in persuading someone else to vote for what the trader most wants, buys this support by casting his own vote against something he (and his constituents) may hold slightly less dear. However nobly inspired such commerce may be, constituents and others may misunderstand it, resenting the vote cast against their interest without appreciating what was bought with it. Naturally, therefore, legislative traders are not eager to talk about potentially misunderstood arrangements.

The main reason actual instances of vote-trading are difficult to identify, however, is that most of them take place in necessarily nonpublic circumstances. Vote-trading is expensive to carry out, especially in large legislatures where significant groups must be persuaded to act in concert to do something that some of them may be disinclined to do. Consequently, in modern legislatures most vote-trading goes on in private in small committees where alternatives can be discussed discreetly and agreements reached in a reasonable amount of time. Thus, in American legislatures, committees write bills in "markup" sessions (usually closed to the public, though no longer so in Congress), and the process of writing is the successive discovery of themes or formulations that satisfy every element of a winning coalition. Naturally, some of the themes are contradictory in spirit: What satisfies group A harms group B, and what satisfies B harms A. Yet, in a well-written bill, both A and B are on balance satisfied because each has been satisfied by desired themes more than harmed by undesired ones. This is, of course, what vote-trading consists of; and it is, to a considerable degree, the informality and privacy of the markup that make the literary effort successful.

One location where vote-trading is clearly visible is, thus, in the record of a secret and relatively small decision-making body. The Philadelphia Convention of 1787 was relatively small (on most days, about forty delegates), left a good record of its discussions (namely, Madison's *Notes*), and was extraordinarily secret—hardly any of its daily details were leaked either in correspondence or casual conversation, and apparently no one out-of-doors (except printers) saw the working papers.* Fortunately, there were a number of implicit and explicit trades and one of them constitutes the example for this essay.

Toward the end of the Convention, two unrelated questions, among others, remained unresolved:
1. Should Congress be authorized to prohibit the slave trade immediately or should it be restrained from prohibition until some later date, say 1800 or 1808? For convenience, let "A" stand for the power of immediate prohibition, and "a" stand for the power of future prohibition.
2. Should Congress be authorized to pass navigation acts (i.e., acts prohibiting foreign ships from loading cargo in American ports) by a simple majority ("B") or by only a two-thirds majority ("b")?
Although the two issues are unrelated, they were brought together into a single dimension of judgment in order to facilitate ratification of the Constitution. What made the junction possible was nothing, I think, inherent in these issues as issues,

---

*The remarkable degree of secrecy in the Convention is suggested in an anecdote written by William Pierce (Ga.). Early in the Convention, members made copies of "propositions brought forward as great leading principles" (probably the Virginia plan). A member dropped his handwritten copy and it was found and picked up by Thomas Mifflin (Pa.), who gave it to Washington as presiding officer. At the end of the day, Washington addressed the Convention thus (as reconstructed by Pierce): "I am sorry to find that some one Member of this Body, has been so neglectful of the secrets of the Convention as to drop in the State House a copy of their proceedings, which by accident was picked up and delivered to me this morning. I must entreat Gentlemen to be more careful, lest our transactions get into the News Papers, and disturb the public repose by premature speculations. I know not whose Paper it is, but there it is (throwing it down on the table), let him who owns it take it." Pierce continued: "At the same time he bowed, picked up his hat, and quitted the room with a dignity so severe that every Person seemed alarmed." Furthermore, Pierce concluded: "It is something remarkable that no Person ever owned the Paper."

but rather the fortunate accident that dominant opinions in the two main regions, North and South, were arranged so that a trade was possible:

Preference Orders of Delegates	Eastern*and Middle†States	Southern‡ States	Virginia
Most desired outcome	AB	ab	Ab
	aB	aB	ab
	Ab	Ab	AB
Least desired outcome	ab	AB	aB

* Eastern: New Hampshire, Massachusetts, Connecticut
† Middle: New Jersey, Pennsylvania, Delaware
‡ Southern: Maryland, North Carolina, South Carolina, Georgia
Note: New York delegates had gone home and Rhode Island did not send delegates.

The foregoing table shows that delegates from the Northern states most of all wanted (AB)—that is, simple majority rule on navigation acts (B) and immediate prohibition of the slave trade (A), and that the simple majority was more important than prohibition. (That is, failing to get their way on both, they would rather have aB than Ab.)

The rationale for this ordering was, first, that the shipping and shipbuilding in Philadelphia, Boston, and all the smaller New England coastal towns, which had been severely restricted during the Revolution, had not subsequently revived because British navigation acts excluded American bottoms from both British and West Indian ports. Consequently, Northern commercial interests were eager to retaliate by prohibiting British ships from ports in the United States. Their hope was, of course, that this retaliation would lead to negotiation and thence to reconciliation and free trade, at least between these nations, as indeed did eventually come about.

The second element of the rationale of the Northern preference was that opinion in many Northern states was, as early as 1787, opposed to slavery and especially to the slave trade. Comparing the two issues, however, that of navigation acts, which touched on pocketbooks, was probably more salient to the Eastern delegations than the issue of slavery, which touched only on souls.

Southern delegates most desired (ab), that is, delay of prohibition to the future (a) and passage of navigation acts by a two-thirds majority (b). Especially by South Carolina and Georgia, rapidly developing states in need of field hands, the opportunity to import slaves freely was thought to be a vital economic interest. A lesser, but still important, economic interest was the two-thirds rule. Most Southerners expected that a navigation act closing Southern ports to foreign ships would increase their shipping costs. But a two-thirds rule, which would require 18 out of 26 senators to carry, would give the five Southern states a veto on navigation acts. Compared with the issue of the importation of slaves, however, the rule on navigation acts was economically trivial, at least for South Carolina and Georgia. Thus, for them (aB) was preferred over (Ab). North Carolina and Maryland delegates were less dependent on importation, however, so their delegates may have preferred (Ab) to (aB).

Virginia was in a strikingly different position, however, which is why I have separated it from the rest of the South. Its staple was tobacco, and its citizens were especially sensitive to shipping costs. At the same time, it had far more slaves than any other state and they were swiftly and naturally increasing. It was indeed to Virginia's advantage to prohibit the importation of slaves because then it would have a monopoly in selling its excess slaves to South Carolina and Georgia. So Virginian delegates, especially George Mason and Governor Randolph, much desired both immediate prohibition (A) and a two-thirds rule (b), though, as we shall see, the two-thirds rule was their main concern (Ab).

Looking at the preference orders of the delegations, it is obvious that a trade was possible. The second-best outcome for both Northern and Southern states was the combination of future prohibition (a) and simple majority (B). Only Virginians, for whom (aB) was the worst outcome, would be severely hurt by the trade. This obvious second best made nearly everybody (but Virginians) pretty happy and so one might reasonably expect the second best to occur, especially since a minority of the Virginia delegation on these issues (certainly Madison and probably Washington) were also quite satisfied with the outcome of a trade (aB).

In a strict sense, no trade was necessary. The six Eastern and Middle states had an absolute majority of the eleven delegations present; so they could have imposed their favored outcome, immediate prohibition and simple majority. But they were convinced, I believe, by the repeated assertions made by Southerners that immediate prohibition would lead South Carolina and Georgia to reject the Constitution absolutely and even to secede from the federation. For the sake of peace and federacy, the Northerners were willing to trade.

One might think of the trade as a regional arrangement. Since the proposed Constitution was already opposed by Rhode Island and New York (and perhaps doubtful in Virginia if navigation acts were easy to pass), certainly it would not be viable in the South if importation were to be immediately prohibited. So a trade between the Eastern and Southern states was thought to be necessary to assure ratification, even though the Eastern and Middle states could have won without a trade in the Convention itself.

Looking backward from today's vantage point, one may criticize the Northern delegates for their trade. But they could not foresee the westward movement of slavery and the Civil War. At least it is to the moral credit of Rufus King, a reluctant vote-trader in 1787, that in 1819 he invented the exact antislavery position used in 1858 to dissolve the moral horror which Jeffersonianism had created over a vast area of the South and West.

Standing in the background of this trade was an earlier compromise on representation, and the form this earlier compromise took led inevitably to a dispute on importation. The greatest issue of the Convention was the argument over whether states would have equal votes in the legislature, as in the Articles. The ultimate compromise on that great issue was equal representation for states in the Senate and proportional

representation in the House. During the shaping of that compromise, one important subsidiary issue was what the representation in the House would be proportional to, one possibility being population, another wealth. If population were to be
the standard, then the further question arose: which people
should be counted, just whites, or both whites and blacks?
Easterners preferred just whites, and Gorham (Mass.) even
argued that the white population itself was a measure of
wealth. South Carolinians wanted blacks and whites counted
equally, for that would greatly amplify the white Southern
voice in the House. If, on the other hand, wealth were to be
counted, how should it be measured? Might white population
be a measure of Northern wealth and black population a measure of Southern wealth?

The compromise was one previously used to calculate state
contributions under the Articles (by the Resolution of 18 April
1783): the count would include "the number of free persons"
(including those indentured, but not including Indians not
taxed) plus "three-fifths of all other persons" (i.e., slaves).
But it was never clear which principle this compromise involved. At the same time (9 July) of the first attempt to appor-
tion the House, Gorham explained that (even without the
three-fifths rule) apportionment was based on "the number of
whites and blacks with some regard to supposed wealth." Later (8 August), with the three-fifths rule in place, it was still
unclear. Gouverneur Morris (Pa.), who of all the framers was
most offended by slavery, asked: "Upon what principle is it
that the slaves shall be computed in the representation? Are
they men? Then make them Citizens and let them vote. Are
they property? Why then is no other property included? . . .
The admission of slaves into the Representation . . . comes to
this: that the inhabitant of Georgia and S.C. who goes to the
Coast of Africa, and in defiance of the most sacred laws of
humanity tears away his fellow creatures from their dearest
connections and damns them to the most cruel bondages, shall
have more votes in a Govt. instituted for the protection of
rights of mankind, than the Citizen of Pa. or N. Jersey who
views with a laudable horror so nefarious a practice."

The issue of what the three-fifths were, other than a Southern advantage, was never satisfactorily resolved until the Thirteenth Amendment (1865). But once the three-fifths formula was accepted in the Convention, Northerners immediately concluded that some kind of limit on importation was necessary. To continue Morris's speech about the "nefarious practice," "What is the proposed compensation to the Northern States for a sacrifice of every principle of right, of every impulse of humanity. They are to bind themselves to march their militia for the defence of the S. States; for their defence agst those very slaves of whom they complain. . . . On the other side the Southern States are not to be restrained for importing fresh supplies of wretched Africans, at once to increase the danger of attack, and the difficulty of defence; nay they are to be encouraged to it by an assurance of having their votes in the Natl. Govt. increased in proportion. . . ."

Such is the origin of the limit on importation. We know much less about the origin of the provision on navigation acts. It was not, apparently, discussed in the first two months of the Convention, and it appears suddenly (6 August) in the Report of the Committee on Detail. From Jefferson's record of a conversation (30 September 1792) with Mason (Va.), it seems that Mason remembered the two-thirds rule on navigation acts as being a central part of the agreement all along. The absence of discussion in Madison's *Notes* thus seems strange, until it is observed that other central issues were also undebated. For example, paper money was only occasionally mentioned until the Report of the Committee on Detail prohibited state bills of credit and legal tender laws. Most historians would agree, however, that one of the framers' main complaints about state legislatures was their proclivity to issue paper money as legal tender. Similarly, the prohibition of state imposts appeared initially in the Report, though the elimination of state tariffs was one of the main objectives of delegates from nonmaritime states. One concludes that the framers, conscious of writing for the future, concentrated on this work rather than on immediate political problems. Probably, however, they, like any other political men, incessantly discussed immediate issues and arrived at resolutions, which then showed up, for the first time in many cases, in the Report of the Committee on Detail.

This report provided, inter alia, in Article VII (VI), Sections 4–6:

Sec. 4, clause 1: "No tax or duty shall be laid by the Legislature on articles exported from any State";

Sec. 4, clause 2: "nor on the migration or importation of such persons as the several States shall think proper to admit";

Sec. 4, clause 3: "nor shall such migration or importation be prohibited";

Sec. 5: "No capitation tax shall be laid, unless in proportion to the Census hereinbefore directed to be taken";

Sec. 6: "No navigation act shall be passed without the assent of two-thirds of the members present in each House.

This was the set of provisions that led to the vote-trade here described.

To understand the trade, it is necessary, I believe, to understand the success of the Southern delegates in persuading the others that some importation of slaves was absolutely essential for ratification in the South. While Virginians and even some delegates from the deep South simply insisted on the rights of slaveholders in general, some Southerners made the real point frequently and bluntly. Williamson (N.C.), in most matters a moderate man, said "The S. States could not be members of the Union if the clause [i.e., Art. VII, Sec. 4, clauses 2 and 3] should be rejected." Charles Cotesworth Pinckney (S.C.), the most active delegate for the slaveholding interest, asserted that without Section 4, "if himself and all his colleagues were to sign the Constitution and use their personal influence, it would be of no avail towards obtaining the assent of their Constituents. S. Carolina and Georgia cannot do without slaves." And John Rutledge (S.C.), the dominant delegate from the deep South, was the bluntest of all: "The true question at present is whether the Southern States shall or shall not be parties to the Union."

The Northern response to these threats was to give in. Some Northerners had given in from the beginning, taking a high moral line against slavery but acquiescing in the slave trade. When George Mason (Va.), the owner of hundreds of slaves, denounced the African (but not, apparently, the domestic) slave trade and declared with amazing unconcern that "every master of slaves is a petty tyrant," Oliver Ellsworth (Conn.) replied rather drily that, "as he had never owned a slave [he] could not judge the effects of slavery on character," and urged that the Convention not "intermeddle" in what he saw as an internal squabble in the South between Virginia, where "slaves . . . multiply so fast . . . it is cheaper to raise than import them," and South Carolina, in the "sickly rice swamps" to which "foreign supplies are necessary."

Other Northerners at first opposed the slave interest in every way, only to capitulate. Wilson (Pa.) initially opposed counting slaves for representation, yet he was the one who proposed the three-fifths rule. King (Mass.) suggested that, if Southern states might leave the Union, so might Northern ones, but he ultimately became a spokesman for the vote-trade. Most astonishing of all was Gouverneur Morris (Pa.) His contempt for defenders of slavery was unbounded, and in this debate, just to embarrass them, he moved that the clause read "importation of slaves into N. Carolina, S. Carolina and Georgia." Once a few slow-witted delegates squirmed to defend the euphemisms, he withdrew his motion. Yet it was Morris, expert heresthetician in spite of himself, who proposed the vote-trade. After clause 1 of Article VII, Section 4, was adopted and debate wrangled on about the next two clauses, he "wished the whole subject to be committed including the clauses relating to taxes on exports and to a navigation act. *These things may form a bargain among the Northern and Southern States*" (emphasis added).

So Sections 4–6 were committed to a committee of eleven (one from each state) and it produced the required trade. This was its proposal (24 August):

> For Section 4, clauses 2 and 3: strike them out and insert "The migration or importation of such persons as the several States now existing shall think proper to admit, shall not be

prohibited by the Legislature prior to the year 1800—but a tax or Duty may be imposed on such migration or importation at a rate not exceeding the average of Duties laid on Imports";
for Section 5 (on capitation taxes): to remain;
for Section 6 (on navigation acts): to be stricken out.

Thus it proposed (aB). And this is what the Convention adopted. The Northern delegates faithfully kept the bargain made in the committee, even though some had been initially dubious. (Massachusetts delegates had been uneasy about committing Sections 4—6 to a committee that would produce a compromise. They may have feared trouble at home if they acquiesced in the slave trade. So, even though all three spoke on 22 August, Massachusetts was "absent" from vote #337, 22 August, on the motion to commit.) The report relative to Section 4 from 24 August was steamrollered through on 25 August, even extending 1800 to 1808 (thus giving South Carolina a full twenty years of unrestrained importation), on motion by C. C. Pinckney (S.C.) and Gorham (Mass.). The vote (#368, 25 August) to adopt the committee report on Section 4 was 7–4, with Massachusetts, New Hampshire, and Connecticut voting with the South.

When it came to the other half of the vote-trade, however, Charles Pinckney (S.C.) objected, proposing to delete that part relating to Section 6 in order to restore the two-thirds rule. But Pinckney was young and brash, and his three senior colleagues systematically rebuked him and in the process explained the full details of the vote-trade. Charles Cotesworth Pinckney revealed the most, so I quote his speech in full.

"Genl. Pinckney said it was the true interest of the S. States to have no regulation of commerce; but considering the loss brought on the commerce of the Eastern States by the revolution, their liberal conduct toward the views of South Carolina" [here Madison inserted a footnote: "He meant the permission to import slaves. An understanding on the two subjects of *navigation* and *slavery* (emphasis in original), had taken place between those parts of the Union, which explains the vote on the

Motion depending, as well as the language of Genl. Pinckney and others."], ". . . and the interest the weak Southern States had in being united with the strong Eastern States, he thought it proper that no fetters should be imposed on the power of making commercial regulations; and that his constituents though prejudiced against the Eastern States, would be reconciled to [i.e., by] this liberality—He had himself, he said, prejudices agst the Eastern States before he came here, but he would acknowledge that he had found them as liberal and candid as any men whatever." So Charles Pinckney's motion to take up the two-thirds rule failed, 7–4, in vote 399, 29 August and (B) was then passed without opposition.

One can see the trade easily thus:

Vote 368		Vote 399	
To agree to the first clause of the report of the committee of eleven		To postpone the third clause of the report of the committee of eleven	
Yea (for a)	Nay (for A)	Yea (for b)	Nay (for B)
N.H. ◄———————			N.H.
Mass ◄———————			Mass.
Conn.◄———————			Conn.
	N.J.		N.J.
	Pa.		Pa.
	Del.		Del.
Md.		Md.	
	Va.	Va.	
N.C.		N.C.	
S.C.		——————————►	S.C.
Ga.		Ga.	

where the arrows indicate the trade-induced votes. Note that only South Carolina voted with the Eastern states on navigation acts, but its vote maintained the integrity of the trade. (Possibly Maryland and North Carolina were not fully committed to the bargain, and Georgia delegates may have believed their vote unnecessary.)

The consequences of the trade were straightforward. The Massachusetts ratifying convention ratified, under intense pressure from shipping interests in coastal towns. Elbridge Gerry, the Massachusetts delegate who refused to sign the Constitution and became an anti-Federalist leader, was not even elected to the Massachusetts convention; and Gerry's mentor, Samuel Adams, was silenced in the convention by the intense enthusiasm of Bostonians. Even though anti-Federalists began with a clear majority of delegates, the Federalists won—in no small part, in my opinion—because of the opportunity for a navigation act.

Similarly, South Carolina ratified—again in no small part—because the slavery issue was settled to slaveowners' satisfaction. In the South Carolina ratifying convention, Charles Cotesworth Pinckney, as extraordinarily candid as in Philadelphia, responded to a criticism of the compromise on importation with a survey of the settlement on slavery: "On this point your delegates had to contend with the religious and political prejudices of the Eastern and Middle States, and with the interested and inconsistent opinion of Virginia, who was warmly opposed to our importing more slaves. . . ." Turning to the vote-trade, he described the Eastern delegates as offering the bargain: " 'Show some period' . . . [they said] 'when it may be in our power to put a stop, if we please, to the importation of this weakness, and we will endeavor, for your convenience, to restrain the religious and political prejudice of our people on this subject.' " Then, without mentioning the rule on navigation acts, he described the committee report and recited the value of the settlement: ". . . we have secured an unlimited importation of negroes for twenty years. Nor is it declared that the importation shall then be stopped; it may be continued. We have a security that the general government can never emancipate them, for no such authority is granted; and it is admitted, on all hands, that the general government has no powers but what are expressly granted by the Constitution. . . . We have obtained a right to recover our slaves in whatever part of America they may take refuge, which is a right we had not before. In short, considering all circumstances, we have made the best terms for the security of this species of property it was in our power to make. We would have made better if we could; but, on the whole, I do not think them bad." Neither did his colleagues, and South Carolina ratified easily.

But what was gained in Massachusetts and South Carolina was almost lost in Virginia. Two of the Virginia delegates refused to sign the Constitution, and in both cases it was the simple majority on navigation acts (B) that turned them away. Randolph said, in the debate on Section 6, "There were features so odious in the Constitution as it stands, that he doubted whether he should be able to agree to it. A rejection of the motion [i.e., to postpone striking out the two-thirds rule] would compleat the deformity of the system. . . ." So the vote-trade was the marginal influence on Randolph's defection, although he was ultimately reconciled and supported the Constitution in the Virginia ratifying convention. Mason, on the other hand, was irreconcilable. As he told Jefferson five years later, it was the vote-trade and the loss of the two-thirds rule that turned him against the Constitution. And out of this parochial and petty economic interest, he fought the Constitution to the bitter end.

The battle in Virginia was very close, but it did ratify. So the judgment of the vote-traders was probably correct. South Carolina and Massachusetts were won and Virginia was not lost. The Constitution was ratified and the Union preserved, but with a terrible blot which it required a civil war to remove. Would it have been better to have no union at all than to have a civil war seventy years later?

Sources: All the detail mentioned here is in Max Farrand, ed., *The Records of the Federal Convention of 1787*, rev. ed., 4 vols. (New Haven: Yale University Press, 1911, 1937, and 1964).

9 HOW TO WIN
ON A ROLL CALL
BY NOT VOTING

Many people equate the art of political manipulation with skill in exploiting the arcane minutiae of parliamentary law. By now the readers of this book know this is not true. Heresthetic consists mainly of inventing sentences, like Lincoln's question or DePew's amendment, and only incidentally involves the simple exploitation of rules, like Pliny's unsuccessful effort to tally votes in an unexpected way. Still, the ability to manipulate rules is occasionally very important, and here is a good example involving one of the most controversial issues of the last decade.

In 1980 the Equal Rights Amendment was defeated in the Virginia Senate by the refusal of a single senator to vote. Had he voted against the amendment, as was his earlier intention, it would have won; but, paradoxically, he was able to defeat it by not voting at all. This maneuver depended on the Virginia rule that required an absolute majority of the senate, rather than a simple majority of those voting, for the passage of a resolution to ratify an amendment to the United States Constitution.

After a careful count of the house on both sides and a switch by one senator in the previous week, it appeared to be certain that the vote would turn out to be tied, 20–20, in the forty-member senate. The rules provided that the lieutenant governor, the presiding officer, break the tie. The lieutenant governor, who was Charles S. Robb, son-in-law of President Johnson, had promised to break the tie in favor of E.R.A., and Lynda Robb, as chairwoman of the President's Advisory Committee on Women had, as her contribution, obtained and distributed the opinion of a former Virginia attorney general justifying Lieutenant Governor Robb's intention. Were all this to occur, that is, the 20–20 tie and the casting vote, the outcome would be 21–20, an absolute majority of the whole senate for E.R.A.

Everything went according to plan until Senator John Chichester, an opponent of E.R.A., refused to vote, invoking a senate rule that permitted a senator to abstain on a roll call involving an issue in which he or she had "an immediate, private or personal interest." It is perhaps hard to imagine what private or personal interest anyone could have on a public resolution like the E.R.A., but Senator Chichester insisted that his personal interest was "my interest in the Commonwealth of Virginia, the people of Virginia." The presiding officer accepted this rationale, though it is hard to say why. Had he been as tough as Pliny, he would have ruled that Chichester must vote. And, had Chichester appealed to the floor, the senate would presumably have sustained Robb by 20 to 19, if Chichester did not vote, or by 21 to 20, if both Chichester and Robb voted. Why was Robb so docile? Perhaps he believed he could not honorably reject Chichester's rationale, for to do so was to guarantee a vote for Robb himself. Perhaps, on the other hand, Robb was less than enthusiastic about E.R.A. and about his wife's efficiency in managing his vote. As a result of Chichester's abstention, the vote was 20 to 19 in favor of E.R.A., not an absolute majority of the whole Senate; so the resolution failed.

What should one say of a rule that brings about this bizarre result? It is easy enough to identify the mathematical explanation: One well-known property of rules for decision is "monotonicity," the feature that the addition of a vote to one side increases, or at least does not decrease, its chance to win. Another property is "neutrality," the feature that the voting rule does not favor any alternative (here, passage or failure to pass). Clearly, the requirement of an absolute majority does not satisfy either property. It violates monotonicity in the sense that, without Chichester's vote his side won, but with it, his side would have lost. It violates neutrality in the sense that it was easier to defeat the resolution than to pass it.

Still, having explained the outcome mathematically, what should be said of the rule morally? Simple majority rule does satisfy monotonicity and neutrality and, had it been the standard of decision here, the E.R.A. would have won, 20 to 19. But does one want to make Constitutional change easy? Perhaps it is better to set the hurdle high for Constitutional amendments, in which case a non-neutral, non-monotonic rule may be justified.

In any event, neither side was prepared to concede. The lieutenant governor was quoted as saying that this was something Chichester would "have to wrestle over with his own conscience," as if it were immoral to use existing rules to win. Mr. Chichester was quoted as saying, with considerable self-satisfaction, "I felt I could best serve the people of Virginia and of my district [Fredricksburg] by not voting at all."

Sources: My knowledge of this event comes from stories in *The Washington Star,* 13 February 1980, p. B-3, under the byline of Zofia Smardz, and *The Washington Post,* 13 February 1980, pp. 1 and 29, under the byline of Karlyn Barker. I owe the comparison with Pliny to James Alt.

10 WARREN MAGNUSON
AND NERVE GAS

Most of the public heresthetical maneuvers I have so far described depended for their success on careful planning or a long campaign. Lincoln's question at Freeport involved both. De-Pew's amendment and Plott and Levine's motions were carefully planned, and Morris's coup on the electoral college derived from his persistent (though flexible) pursuit of a well-articulated goal. But not all heresthetical success involves great issues or careful planning or long-term hopes and ambitions. Accomplished herestheticians maneuver every day as part of their ordinary business. The protagonist of this chapter, Senator Warren Magnuson, was just such a day laborer in the heresthetical vineyard, and the story I will tell involves only a morning's work of winning on a motion by introducing a second dimension of judgment. Magnuson himself probably soon forgot his triumph, and his practiced skill was so smoothly displayed that most observers probably continued to think of him as just an ordinary senator, more remarkable for holding his office than for using it. Still the heresthetical achievement in this event, though only a cameo, is a sculpture of gemlike brilliance and enduring beauty.

During the Vietnam War, when nearly everything the military did was subject to heresthetical attack, the Defense Department, probably itself attempting a heresthetical maneuver, determined to repatriate and detoxify a substantial portion of its chemical warfare supplies—Operation Red Hat. The plan was that some shells were to be chemically destroyed, some were to be dumped at sea, and some that were stored in other countries were to be returned for storage or detoxifying in the United States. Since some shells of nerve gas were stored in

Okinawa, Japan, this plan necessitated shipping them home. Incidentally, the previous year about two dozen American soldiers on Okinawa were treated for nerve-gas injuries and this event revealed to both American and Japanese citizens the existence of storage on the island. Quite probably, this too was an important part of the reason for Operation Red Hat.

It was initially proposed that the Okinawan gas be brought through the port of Seattle for rail shipment to the Umatilla Army Depot in Oregon. Nerve gas is a frightening thing and, if the possibility were publicly (and perhaps heresthetically) raised that the gas might escape from the shells, then many otherwise indifferent people in Washington and Oregon could reasonably be expected to object. Naturally, politicians in the Northwest were dismayed and Senator Magnuson presented an amendment, on 21 May 1970, to a pending military authorization bill (the Foreign Military Sales bill) to add: "No funds authorized or appropriated pursuant to this Act or any other law may be used to transport chemical munitions from Okinawa to the United States."

Joining Magnuson in sponsoring this amendment were Henry Jackson (Dem.), the senior senator from Washington, both of the Oregon senators (both Republicans) and Senator Mike Gravel of Alaska (Dem.)—altogether an impressive coalition from the Northwest, rendered especially strong by the fact that Jackson, the "Senator from Boeing," was a hawkish and valuable friend of the Pentagon.

Magnuson explained to the Senate that he was afraid of the very act of shipment: "the real danger comes in the process of transit, . . . being unloaded . . . in the United States, and then loaded into railway cars for a lengthy trip through an area heavily populated with people who are very upset about this activity"—doubtless, furthermore, upset in part, as he intended them to be, by the very speech he as a Democratic senator was then making to discredit a Republican administration. Rhetorically Magnuson asked: "The movement plan involves nearly a full month of constant presence within Washington State of trains moving with this awful cargo. How can we assure that some deranged or misguided person will not

provoke an incident that could set off a tragedy unparalleled in
our history?" Most of all, he could not understand why the
nerve gas should not be left in Okinawa (though doubtless
Okinawans could understand): "What is the use of moving it?
No one wants it in this country. It is already stored in Okinawa. I saw that storage area in Okinawa last September. No
one seemed very concerned about it. They have truck gardens
over the storage area where they are raising turnips and
onions."

Probably as a result of the furor raised by the sponsors of
the amendment, the Defense Department decided not to bring
nerve gas into the "continental United States," which, as Magnuson subsequently reported, did not exclude shipment to
Alaska, specifically to the Kodiak Naval Station. So Senator
Mike Gravel of Alaska produced, on 29 June 1970, an alternative to Magnuson's amendment: "No funds authorized or appropriated pursuant to this or any other law may be used to
transport chemical munitions from the Island of Okinawa to
the United States. Such funds as are necessary for the detoxifi-
cation or destruction of the above described chemical munitions are hereby authorized and shall be used for the detoxifi-
cation or destruction of chemical munitions outside the United
States." The intent of this motion was to force the Defense
Department to decommission the shells on the island of Okinawa itself.

Magnuson's great heresthetical maneuver was in support of
Gravel's amendment. The maneuver is well described by Eric
Redman, who served for two years on Magnuson's staff and
wrote a revealing (though regrettably starry-eyed and naive)
book about his experiences. Magnuson had asked Redman for
a summary of arguments against the shipment, to be used in
floor debate on Gravel's amendment. Redman prepared a
summary of previous arguments like those about trains. Then
he was quite "bewildered" because, just before the debate,
Magnuson studied it "cursorily" and rejected it with "an an-
noyed 'no, no, no.' " When the time came for Magnuson to
speak, he said very little about the parochial complaints of the
Northwest. He instinctively understood, as Redman had not,

that no new support was to be gained by reiterating the old arguments. A new and broader appeal was needed to woo friends of the administration and friends of the Pentagon to vote against Operation Red Hat. (To illustrate just how difficult this was, consider that Henry Jackson, Magnuson's senior colleague and partisan ally, might, superficially, have been expected to vote to keep nerve gas out of the Northwest. But Jackson, who was a good friend of the Defense Department, actually voted against Gravel's amendment—that is, for Operation Red Hat—once the danger to Washington state itself had been averted.)

Magnuson's new argument brought an entirely new dimension into the debate, namely the role of the Senate in foreign affairs. This subject was much on the minds of senators at the moment because of the pending Church-Cooper amendment, the consuming issue of the month. It was intended as an anti-administration, anti–Vietnam War measure to cut off funds for military activity in Cambodia. Furthermore, there existed a recent (5 November 1969) Senate resolution relating the constitutional issue of senatorial consent to Okinawa particularly. This resolution, introduced by Harry Byrd (Dem., Va.) and passed 63–14 in the Senate, provided that the president could not change the status of any territory involved in the peace treaty with Japan without the advice and consent of the Senate. Though this amendment had been excised from the State Department appropriations bill in conference (on the ground that is belonged in a substantive bill, not an appropriations bill), there could be no doubt that it expressed the deep sense of the Senate, and, furthermore, Strom Thurmond (Rep., S.C.) had recently (7 April 1970) reviewed the history of the Byrd resolution in a speech in the Senate.

Magnuson's new argument was that Operation Red Hat (though concerned with nerve gas everywhere) was the President's device to avoid consultation with the Senate about Okinawa and the peace treaty with Japan, and thus was also a violation of the (unadopted) Byrd amendment and even of the Constitution itself.

"The administration," Magnuson argued, "never came up to

the Senate to tell us what they were going to do in relation to
Japan or Okinawa. . . . [They claimed] no new treaty was being considered. President Nixon has said . . . that we were
going to remove weapons from Okinawa; . . . but mention
was made only of nuclear weapons. I have looked through
everything and do not find that the Senate was told this involved chemical gas as well."

Having implanted the suggestion that secret decisions had
been made and never reported, Magnuson went on specifically
to apply the Byrd amendment. "The Senate passed," he
pointed out, "a resolution introduced by the Senator from
Virginia, declaring that before the President made any disposi-
tion of Okinawa, he should come to the Senate. That date was
not long ago, some 4 or 5 weeks, I believe [actually eight
months, though Thurmond's review was eleven weeks]. But
the resolution was completely ignored. In the meantime, this
agreement on nerve gas was made. . . . It was an agreement of
great importance about which the Senate was not consulted. It
comes close to being, if it is not in fact, an unconstitutional
usurpation of the Senate's power to ratify treaties."

No longer was Gravel's amendment a parochial concern of
the Northwest. Now, through Magnuson's heresthetic, it involved the prerogatives of the United States Senate. Once
such an issue is raised, it cannot be ignored. Redman tells us
that, owing to Magnuson's clever reformulation of the dimensions of the issue, Gravel's amendment, "which had been
doomed a few minutes earlier, passed overwhelmingly."

Redman exaggerated—the amendment passed 52–40 (including live pairs, with eight absent and unpaired). Since 51 is
a bare constitutional majority, 52 is hardly "overwhelming."
But still, he is essentially correct that Magnuson's reformulation did the trick.

Initially Magnuson had on his side: (1) The regional senators
(that is, those from Washington, Oregon, Idaho, Alaska, and
Hawaii). These totaled nine votes—excluding the backsliding
Jackson—divided into four Democrats and five Republicans.
Seven of these fit equally well into the next category, but I
count them here both to show how small the regional motiva-

tion was by itself and to emphasize that it was the main concern of these senators. (2) Anti-administration forces. I count here all those who voted in favor of both the Gravel amendment and the Church-Cooper amendment. (Church-Cooper, cutting off funds for military operations in Cambodia, was clearly anti-administration.) This category includes 40 senators (29 Democrats, almost all Northern, who would be likely to vote at every opportunity to embarrass the administration in the conduct of the war; and eleven Republicans, all identified with the so-called moderate wing of the party, men like Senators Percy of Illinois, Brooke of Massachusetts, Mathias of Maryland, and Case of New Jersey, who constantly faced the threat of strong Democratic opposition in elections). Of the nine regionally concerned senators, seven (four Democrats and three Republicans) overlap with the anti-administration category. Hence I include only 33 senators in this second category. In the two categories together, there were 42 easy votes for Gravel's amendment.

On the other side, clearly opposed to Gravel and Magnuson, were the 24 senators who voted no on both Gravel and Church-Cooper, plus one more who voted no on Gravel and was absent without a pair on Church-Cooper. These were, for the most part, pro-administration Republicans (17), including Strom Thurmond (S.C.), who had recently reviewed the history of the Byrd amendment, and Southern Democrats (eight), including even Harry Byrd (Va.), on whose resolution Magnuson had built his argument. (Thurmond and Byrd, at least, were unmoved by Magnuson's heresthetic.)

The remainder (33) were the ones from whom Magnuson might expect to get votes. Since, as it turned out, seven were absent and unpaired for the vote on the Gravel amendment, Magnuson's room for maneuver was reduced to 26. Of these, he had to win over at least nine to guarantee passage.

The marginal 26 may be divided into two groups, both of which were essentially supporters of the administration. The first group, call them "Church-Cooper supporters," consisted of those who, though basically pro-administration, wished to rebuke it for the invasion of Cambodia, either out of genuine revulsion or as a device to quiet the public outcry. They were not impressed by Magnuson's heresthetic, which they probably saw as merely a diversionary tactic. The typical senator in this group is Cooper himself (Republican, Ky.). The second group—call them "supporters of prerogative"—consisted of those who supported the administration on Church-Cooper (i.e., voted against it) but who were indeed moved by Magnuson's heresthetic, even though they probably recognized it for what it was, namely a tactic to manipulate them.

Magnuson had no chance with the Church-Cooper supporters. They were sympathetic with the goals of Operation Red Hat (even if the goals were no more than the reduction of criticism of the military). So they would vote no on Gravel, and yes on Church-Cooper. As it turned out, 16 of the 26 were in this category, eleven Democrats, mostly Southern and border, but including Jackson (Wash.), and four Republicans.

Magnuson's support had to come from the supporters of prerogative. They stood fast with the administration on the main issue (by voting no on Church-Cooper), but they also responded to Magnuson's invention of the constitutional issue. There were ten of these, six Republicans like Senators Goldwater (Ariz.) and Scott (Pa.), the minority leader, and four Democrats (three Southern). They probably all understood that Magnuson's appeal was a heresthetical trick, but they probably also believed that, when the constitutional right of the Senate was at stake, it had to be defended.

Along with the 42 regional and anti-administration votes, these ten votes, presumably motivated by the constitutional issue, did the trick. As noted, the Gravel amendment won 52–40. Had these ten votes not been activated, they would have gone to the anti-Gravel forces and the amendment would have lost 42–50. In that sense, Magnuson's introduction of a second dimension carried the day.

This is heresthetic at its best. When the issue was framed in one dimension, approval or disapproval of Operation Red Hat, those who caviled at the method while approving the goal probably could not hope to win. But when the dimension of senatorial consent was added, ten marginal votes were won. I think it quite unlikely that anyone was persuaded by Magnuson's rhetoric, which was ordinary. What swung them over was the two-dimensional structure that required them to defend the Senate, skeptical though they may have been of Magnuson's motives and allegations. Magnuson did not persuade, I think, but maneuvered so that those who would have lost in one dimension won in two. Surely, credit for the victory goes to the heresthetician who thought up the second dimension.

Sources: This story was pointed out to me by Richard Smith, who used it as a running example in his doctoral dissertation, "Lobbying Influence in Congress: Processes and Effects" (University of Rochester, 1980). The story was told first, but quite inaccurately because he wrote from memory, by Eric Redman, *The Dance of Legislation* (New York: Simon and Schuster, 1973), p. 207. My quotations are from the *Congressional Record,* vol. 116, pt. 12, pp. 16481–82 (21 May 1970), and vol. 116, pt. 16, pp. 22016, 22021 (29 June 1970).

11 EXPLOITING THE POWELL AMENDMENT

Some heresthetical maneuvers involve formulating and reformulating issues so that others are, willy nilly, forced to react to the manipulator's advantage. Such maneuvers, as carried through by Lincoln, DePew, or Magnuson, require both acute perception and creativity beyond that of ordinary men. But other heresthetical maneuvers are simpler because they involve no more than using one's vote to channel one's opponents toward a desired outcome. Pliny's adversary did that simply by moving across the room; Chichester did it merely by abstaining on the E.R.A.; more elaborately, the delegates from New England and South Carolina did it by trading votes. The most elaborate such procedures, though still easy to understand, are those in which some voters arrange an intermediate decision in such a way that others are forced to contribute to the final decision that the manipulators want. This is, of course, what DePew's motion did; but it required a remarkable literary effort. Sometimes, as in the story I am going to tell, the motion is freely given to the heresthetician and he has merely to exploit it.

But exploitation is not always easy. Some herestheticians seem to be able to take advantage of opportunities, others not. In the story of this chapter, some legislators triumphed by strategic voting, while others went down to defeat because they consciously avoided (or were constrained from) voting strategically.

To clarify the situation, suppose a decision-making body uses customary parliamentary procedure to edit a sentence with the intention, eventually, of approving or disapproving it. In this process, the body must have before it, at very least:

x, an amendment, which is the potential editorial substitution;
y, an original motion, which is the first draft of a sentence; and
z, the status quo, which is the state of affairs that will prevail if the body rejects the sentence, either as originally proposed or as edited.

With these alternatives, the editing process must, as portrayed in figure 1, go through exactly one of four potential histories:

FIGURE 1

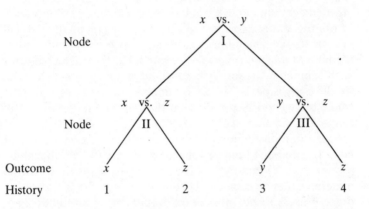

1. In the choice at node I, between the amendment and the original, the amendment (x) wins. Then, pitted at node II against the status quo, the amended motion wins, so x is the final outcome. This is the history made by choosing the left path at nodes I and II.
2. In the choice, at node I, between the amendment and the original, the amendment wins. Then, pitted at node II against the status quo (z) the amended motion loses, so z is the final outcome. This is the history made by choosing the left path at node I and the right path at node II.
3. In the choice, at node I, between the amendment and the original, the original (y) wins. Then, pitted at node III against the status quo, the original again wins, so y is the final outcome. This is the history made by choosing the right path at node I and the left path at node III.
4. In the choice, at node I, between the amendment and the original,

the original wins. Then, pitted at node III against the status quo (z), the original loses so z is the final outcome. This is the history made by choosing the right path at nodes I and III.

Suppose one wanted to predict which one of these potential histories would actually occur. Could one do so? I think not, even if one knew the preferences of all the members of the voting body. Here is a scenario in which prediction is well nigh impossible. Suppose there are an odd number of members and at node I (where the amendment is put against the original) the split between all the members but one is a tie. Then the remaining member, call him M, can cast the deciding vote. Suppose M favors the status quo most of all and then prefers the original motion to the amendment, that is, z to y to x—and z to x. Member M might be expected to vote for y, the original, against x, the amendment, simply because he prefers y to x. If he does so, the body is put at node III. Suppose further that, at III, the whole body chooses y over z, so the original motion wins. But suppose again that, if the body were ever at node II, it would choose the status quo, z, over the amendment, x. If so, then at node I, member M might vote for x against y (even though he prefers y to x) simply in order to get to node II, which he prefers, rather than node III. (Node II is preferable to M because it leads to his most desired outcome, z, the status quo, while node III leads to y, his second-best outcome.)

Let us call voting for x (in the hope of getting z) "strategic" voting and for y "nonstrategic" voting. Since strategic voting leads to M's best outcome, one might expect strategic voting to occur. But if M's constituents think voting for x is in itself evil, then one might expect nonstrategic voting. It seems entirely unclear what might happen in this situation.

This scenario may seem contrived, but is merely a slight abstraction of the event I will now describe. The most interesting feature of this event is that at least two groups of members had the opportunity to vote strategically, but only one group did so. That only one chose to vote strategically is strong evidence of the difficulty of prediction, even though it is possible to specify everyone's preference order quite accurately.

The story I have to tell involves a bill for federal aid to education, a bill sponsored by the Democratic leadership of the House of Representatives in 1956. (It was clearly not a bill put forward by the administration, which was of course Republican.) The bill authorized the distribution of federal funds to the states for the purpose of building schools. The motive for this proposal was straightforward: this was ten years into the baby boom of 1946–62, so that schools were being filled up rapidly. Many state and local officials wanted help in school building. And the Democratic leadership apparently believed it was advantageous to provide the help, or at least to make the gesture in an election year.

Several amendments were proposed on the House floor, but Adam Clayton Powell, a black representative from Harlem, offered the crucial one. It provided that grants could be given only to states with schools "open to all children without regard to race in conformity with the requirements of the United States Supreme Court decisions," a reference to the case of *Brown v. Board of Education* (1954), in which the Court had declared racial segregation in schools to be unconstitutional.

The Powell amendment posed dilemmas for two kinds of Democrats. For Southern Democrats, the unamended bill was attractive because it would doubtless bring more money into their districts than it would take out in taxes. The South was then still a net exporter of people and a net importer of federal dollars. But, if amended, the bill would both deny aid and tax their districts for Northern benefits. Furthermore, it would increase the threat to their institutions of racial segregation. For urban Northern Democrats and Republicans with substantial numbers of black voters in their districts, the bill as amended by the Powell amendment was attractive as a symbol and as a method of diverting federal largess to Northern metropolitan areas. But, if amended, the bill promised to repel Southern Democrats, whose defection would probably defeat it. In sum, Northern urban representatives liked the bill only if amended and Southern Democrats liked it only if not amended. All of this would have made no difference if the bill could have passed easily. But this was not the case. Many Republicans opposed the bill, not only because it increased the federal budget, but also and perhaps mainly because it increased the federal presence in local government. (Up to that time, the federal government had never given direct general financial aid to local schools, although it had financed special programs like vocational education.) Consequently, the Democratic dilemma had a significant effect on the fate of the bill.

There were two relevant roll calls: (1) a vote on adding the Powell amendment, which passed; and (2) a vote on the passage of the amended bill, which failed. The totals (including live pairs) on the two roll calls intersect thus:

| | | Final Passage | | |
		Yea	Nay	Totals
Powell Amendment	Yea	132	97	229
	Nay	67	130	197
	Totals	199	227	426

This table generates four groups based on voting records (yea/yea, yea/nay, nay/yea, nay/nay), which correspond closely with four identifiable natural groups based on shared political attitudes.

To interpret these attitudes, one can construct individual (and group) preference orders out of the alternatives before the House. These alternatives, the set $C = \{x,y,z\}$ of components of possible outcomes, were:

  x: the bill with the Powell amendment;
  y: the original, unamended bill;
  z: the status quo, i.e., no action.

These alternatives can be arranged in six possible orders (xyz, xzy, yxz, . . . , zxy), five of which were the preference orders of natural political groups.

Consider those who voted Y/Y. On the second roll call (where strategic voting was impossible) they voted for x over

$z.$* This limits their possible preference orders to xyz, xzy and yxz. On the first roll call they voted for x over y. If they voted nonstrategically, then yxz is also impossible. (Furthermore, if they preferred y to x, then to vote for x over y is exactly the wrong way to get y. Since y was more likely to beat z than was x, to vote for x would also help get the worst outcome in yxz.) So we eliminate yxz for this group, leaving xzy or xyz. I think xzy is highly unlikely for the Democrats. To have held xzy one would have wanted school aid only if the Powell amendment were adopted—that is, only if the South were deprived of aid. Considering the intensity of the Democratic leadership's commitment to the bill and the cultural norm of getting along by going along, it seems unlikely that any Democrat had this dog-in-the-manger preference order. Of course, some Republicans might have wanted school aid confined to the North, but even if the preferences of all the 54 Y/Y Republicans are reversed from xyz to xzy, it makes no difference in this case to the outcome between y and z. For convenience, we can therefore say that all the Y/Y voters had xyz as their ordering.

This was a natural political group, mostly Northern urban, and fairly closely divided (60 percent-40 percent) between Democrats and Republicans. Sixty-six percent of the 78 Y/Y Democrats were from New England and the big cities of the Midwest and Middle Atlantic states (only 38 percent of the 227 Democrats voting on these roll calls were from this region). Similarly, 65 percent of the 54 Y/Y Republicans were from New England, New York, New Jersey, and Pennsylvania (while only 32 percent of the 199 Republicans voting on these roll calls were from the same states). It seems clear that the Y/Y voters mainly represented Northern urban districts. Presumably, Democrats and Republicans from this region were vying with each other for identification with the interests of blacks as interpreted by Adam Clayton Powell. I will call this group the Powellians.

Those who voted N/Y clearly preferred x to z on the second

---

*At the last roll call, strategic voting—which involves setting the scene for a later roll call—is impossible simply because there *is* no later roll call.

roll call, where voting reveals nonstrategic preferences; so, like the Powellians, they might have xyz, xzy, or yxz. Since we have eliminated xzy and attributed xyz to the Powellians, this leaves only yxz for the N/Y voters, if they voted nonstrategically. They also are a natural political group, the people who preferred school aid to anything else. The 42 N/Y Democrats (only 19 percent of the Democrats voting) were the regulars, who followed the party leadership. The 24 N/Y Republicans were presumably those (from states like Maine, Washington, and Colorado) who preferred school aid to a gesture for blacks, though they were not adamantly opposed to the gesture and preferred it to no action. I will call this group the school-aiders.

Those who voted N/N (107 Democrats and 23 Republicans) are clearly identifiable. They were all the Southern and most of the border Democrats and Republicans, with a tiny scattering of Northern Democrats and Republicans. Since the N/N voters clearly preferred z to x (because they so voted on the final division where strategic voting is impossible), it follows that their only possible preference orders were zxy, zyx, or yzx. Consider, first, zxy: If this were the true preference order of N/N voters, then their nonstrategic votes would be Y/N (i.e., yea on attaching x to y). Conceivably, however, they voted N/N strategically, while holding zxy. But this does not make sense for people who, as indicated by their placing z first, want most of all to defeat federal aid. To vote N on attaching the Powell amendment (i.e., for y against x) is to increase the chance of the bill ultimately passing. Surely, people who place z first do not want to do that. So the preference order zxy is not possible for N/N voters. At most, N/N voters could have held zyx or yzx, both of which are compatible with nonstrategic N/N votes. For the 116 N/N Southerners (105 Democrats and 11 Republicans), their true preferences were probably yzx, that is, they preferred the unamended bill (y) to the status quo (z), even though they were ultimately constrained to vote nay on the final passage because the bill had been amended (x). A sentiment for y over z was attributed to Southerners both by the House Democratic leadership and the Republicans against school aid. If the attribution was correct, then the 116 Southern N/N voters must have had *yzx*. As for the 14 N/N Northerners (2 Democrats and 12 Republicans), they may have held either *yzx* (like the Southerners) or *zyx*. If the N/N Northerners held *zyx*, then they simply wished to oppose the Powell amendment and the bill itself, whether amended or not. If these were their opinions, it might make more sense to vote strategically (Y/N) to attach the Powell amendment and thus make the bill more vulnerable. Still a few persons may have found the Powell amendment so distasteful that they voted against it even though that action presumably conflicted with the most efficient attainment of their larger purpose. (Indeed, N/N voters with *zyx* preferences were, if they existed, the exact opposite of the Powellians, who were Y/Y voters with *xyz* preferences). I think it likely that all N/N voters, North and South, held *yzx;* but even if some Northerners did not, the numbers are so small that they make no difference in this case. I will therefore refer to N/N voters as Southerners.

The 97 Y/N voters were all Republicans and were thus clearly identifiable with a natural political group, namely Republicans against school aid. Their preference orders may have been either of the remaining unassigned, *zxy* or *zyx*. Clearly, their first preference was to defeat the bill, but they might have had either *xy* or *yx* in the second and third places. If they had *zxy*, which means that they wanted the symbolism of equal treatment for blacks but still preferred no school aid to anything else, then they voted directly in accord with their preference orderings. If, on the other hand, they had *zyx*, which means they found the symbolism of the Powell amendment less attractive than the aid bill itself, then they voted strategically, that is, in favor of a less preferred alternative against a more preferred alternative at the first division in order to attain the best attainable outcome at the final division.

It is difficult to decide between these possibilities. The issue really turns on whether or not these Republicans wanted to support desegregation symbolically. Certainly, some, like the New England and New York Republicans, were attached to traditional Republican values of sympathy with black aspirations. On the other hand, most Northern blacks had by 1956 become Democrats, and hence outside the New York and New England area very few Republicans felt obliged to black voters. Representative Bolling, a Democratic whip, put forward Harry Truman to argue the cause of the Democratic leadership. Truman clearly implied that he believed they ordered zyx. Of course, intensely partisan Democrats like Truman and Bolling are hardly good judges of Republican preferences. Still, no Republican bothered to deny Truman's rather maliciously stated allegations. Furthermore, some of those Republicans who voted for the Powell amendment later in the session voted against civil rights measures, which implies an ordering of zyx in this case. Without being able to prove anything numerically, I believe it is reasonable to divide the Republicans in the Y/N category in half, 49 with zxy and 48 with zyx.

Summarizing, then, we have:

132 Powellians (78 Democrats and 54 Republicans), Y/Y, $xyz;$
67 School-aiders (42 Democrats and 25 Republicans), N/Y, $yxz;$
130 Southerners (107 Democrats and 23 Republicans), N/N, $yzx;$
49 Republicans against aid, Y/N, $zxy;$
48 Republicans against aid, Y/N, $zyx.$

With this summary, it is possible to imagine ourselves in the position of congressmen before these votes were taken, as if one were at node I in figure 1. At node I, the motion is to amend the bill, y, with the Powell amendment, x. Whichever one survives, the amended bill at node II or the unamended bill at node III, faces the status quo, z.

A congressman looking forward to the vote could have seen that, if everyone voted according to the preferences previously listed (i.e., nonstrategically), then y would win at node I thus:

	x	vs.	y	
Powellians, xyz	132			
School aiders, yxz			67	(1)
Southerners, yzx			130	
Republicans against aid, zxy	49			
Republicans against aid, zyx			48	
Totals	181		245	

Then, at node III, y would defeat z thus:

	y	vs.	z	
Powellians, xyz	132			
School aiders, yxz	67			(2)
Southerners, yzx	130			
Republicans against aid, zxy or zyx			97	
Totals	329		97	

So the process would be history 3 of figure 1, the outcome would be y, and the bill would pass.

It could also have been seen, however, that those Republicans with zyx preference could defeat the bill by voting strategically—that is, as if they ordered zxy. At node I, instead of voting for y, they could vote for x, so that x rather than y would win, thus:

	x	vs.	y	
Powellians, xyz	132			
School aiders, yxz			67	(3)
Southerners, yzx			130	
Republicans against aid, zxy or zyx	97			
Totals	229		197	

Then at node II, with x facing z, the Republicans holding zyx could vote for z according to their preference orders, so z would win thus:

	x vs.	z	
Powellians, xyz	132		
School aiders, yxz	67		(4)
Southerners, yzx		130	
Republicans against aid, zxy or zyx		97	
Totals	199	227	

So the process would follow history 2 in figure 1 and the outcome would be z, the status quo. Assuming everyone else voted nonstrategically, this group of Republicans holding zyx could produce victory for z by voting for x (their third choice) against y (their second choice). Historically, this is what happened.

But it need not have been so. The Powellians could also have voted strategically, as if they preferred yxz, just like the school-aiders. If they had done so, they could have guaranteed victory for y, their second choice, rather than z, their third choice, no matter how the Republicans against aid voted at node I:

If Powellians had voted strategically and Republicans holding zyx voted:

| | Nonstrategically | | or Strategically | | |
	x vs.	y	x vs.	y	
Powellians, xyz		132		132	
School aiders, yxz		67		67	(5)
Southerners, yzx		130		130	
Republicans against aid, zxy	49		49		
Republicans against aid, zyx	–	48	48		
Totals	49	377	97	329	

Then, at node III all but the Republicans against aid would vote for y against z (as in calculation (2) above), the process would be history 3 with outcome y, and the bill would pass.

All this rather tortuous reasoning can be summarized and depicted graphically by applying an algorithm by Richard McKelvey and Richard Niemi so that all possibilities for strategic voting will be brought into the calculation, as in the righthand comparison in calculation (5). The algorithm is based on the fact that, in the ultimate stage of voting (here, either node II or node III in figure 1), everyone is motivated to vote in strict accord with their preferences. Hence, the certain winners at this stage can easily be identified by summing preferences for each alternative. The winning alternatives can then be treated as the strategic equivalents of their respective nodes. The penultimate stage (node I) now becomes the ultimate stage, and strategic voting is equivalent to a nonstrategic choice between the strategic equivalents of the succeeding nodes. Again, the winner is easily identified (and is the strategic equivalent of node I). Thus, by mathematical induction, one rises up from the lowest level of nodes to the highest, at which point the strategic equivalent is the winner under strategic voting. Since strategic voting consists of choosing one path down the tree over another, this process incorporates all the chances voters have to make such choices. Thus, while using only nonstrategic vote-counts, it gets the result of strategic voting by all the potentially strategic voters.

In this case, at node II the strategic equivalent is z, which is discovered by calculation (4), and at node III it is y, which is discovered by calculation (2). At node I, then, the strategic choice is between node II and node III strategic equivalents, z and y, respectively, of which the winner is y, again by calculation (2). So y is the winner when every potential strategic voter actually votes strategically, as on the right side in calculation (5).

In this case, as in many others, the winning alternative under completely nonstrategic and completely strategic voting is the same. Variations in outcome then occur, as in this case, because, for so far inexplicable reasons, only some voters vote strategically. Here the status quo, z, won in outcome (2) because just the Republicans holding zyx voted strategically. The Powellians could have obtained their second-best, rather than their worst, alternative if they had also been willing to vote strategically. They refused to do so, even though the situation was fully explained to them by the Democratic leadership. Representative Bolling, a Democratic whip, obtained ex-President

Truman's signature on a letter outlining the exact parliamentary situation:

> The Powell amendment raises some very difficult questions. I have no doubt that it was put forward in good faith to protect the rights of our citizens. However, it has been seized upon by the House Republican leadership, which has always been opposed to Federal aid to education, as a means of defeating Federal aid and gaining political advantage at the same time. I think it would be most unfortunate if the Congress should fall into the trap which the Republican leadership has thus set. That is what would happen if the House were to adopt the Powell amendment. The result would be that no Federal aid legislation would be passed at all, and the losers would be our children of every race and creed in every State in the Union.

Despite this persuasive explanation, only one black Democratic congressman, William Dawson, the dean of the black delegation, voted with the leadership. All the rest, and most Northern urban Democrats and Republicans, voted nonstrategically and thus obtained their worst outcome.

Why did this happen?

One explanation, which I reject, is that Republicans against school aid were coolly rational herestheticians who could act for their best advantage, while the Powellians were warm-hearted demonstrators whose emotions prevented rational behavior. It is, however, hard to describe one group as expert herestheticians and the other as fools when both groups experienced the same environment and had often previously acted with each other. So I believe, on the contrary, that all the Powellians, including and especially Adam Clayton Powell himself, were coolly rational calculators who chose, for reasons of rational advantage, to forego influence over the outcome.

My problem, then, is to explain why one set of politicians rationally voted strategically and another set rationally voted nonstrategically. To begin, I note that representatives can earn credit with, and future votes from, people in their constituencies in two distinct ways. One is by producing legislative outcomes that some constituents desire. The other is to take positions of which some constituents approve. When these two techniques of earning credit involve voting differently on the same roll call (as in this story), a representative must calculate which of the actions is the more valuable. Clearly, the Powellians decided that "taking a stand," a highly visible action, would win them more credit in this case than would a future flow of federal dollars into their districts. Contrariwise, the Republicans against school aid made exactly the opposite calculation. If they disliked the symbolism of the Powell amendment yet voted for it, they in effect had decided that stopping the flow of dollars from the federal fisc was far more attractive than the cost of the symbol of the amendment. So people on one side voted for a symbol, people on the other side for an outcome; but on both sides they voted rationally.

Some sense of the relative costs may perhaps be captured from the location in preference orders of the alternatives that had to be supported. The Republicans with zyx had, in order to obtain their best, z, only to vote for their worst, x, against their second-best, y. The Powellians, with xyz, had, in order to obtain at most their second-best, y, to vote against their very best, x. The Republicans with zyx were playing with alternatives that meant relatively little to them, while the Powellians, in order to vote strategically, had to deny what they held dearest. The Republicans against aid were thus able to vote strategically at a low price, while the Powellians would have had to pay a high price.

This story points an important moral: not all people at any one time can act heresthetically and not all leaders can always be successful heresthet-icians. Here the Republicans against school aid were well organized to exploit the situation, and they made the most of their chance to behave heresthetically. The Powellians and the Democratic leadership, however, could at best adapt to the situation in which they found themselves, a situation constructed by Adam Clayton Powell, who was here the best heresthetician of all.

Powell's motive was, undoubtedly, to force some representatives to stand up for the symbolism he created. He probably cared little about federal aid, but he surely cared a lot about the status of blacks. His amendment said to the Democratic leader-

ship, "We blacks must be treated with dignity." His true opponents were thus the border-state Democratic politicians who,
with a kind of offhand contempt for black ambitions, urged
Powellians to vote strategically to mollify the Southern Democrats. The amendment is a display of Powell's own contempt for
Bolling and the Democratic caucus; and Powell's achievement
was to force a large number of other Democrats to join with
him in humiliating Bolling. Doubtless a good number of the
Democratic Powellians felt maneuvered by Powell; and
Bolling's act of trotting out Truman was an effort to extricate
them from the position in which Powell had put them. It was
one heresthetic maneuver against another. Powell's worked and
Bolling's failed. (In other circumstances, however, Bolling was
a good heresthetician—pompous and self-righteous, perhaps,
but clever.) As for the rank and file of the Powellians and the
regular Democrats, they were simply maneuvered by one or the
other heresthetician. These back-benchers for the moment had
to weigh for themselves the merits of following Powell or
Bolling, and they rationally chose to vote strategically or nonstrategically as their several situations indicated.

Sources: I have told this story several times before, first in
"Arrow's Theorem and Some Examples of the Paradox of
Voting," in John Claunch, ed., *Mathematical Applications in
Political Science I* (Dallas: The Arnold Foundation, Southern
Methodist University Press, 1965), pp. 41–60, and most re-
cently in *Liberalism Against Populism: A Confrontation be-
tween the Theory of Democracy and the Theory of Social
Choice* (San Francisco: W. H. Freeman, 1982), pp. 152–56,
and in Arthur T. Denzau, William H. Riker, and Kenneth A.
Shepsle, "Farquharson and Fenno: Sophisticated Voting and
Home Style," *American Political Science Review* 79 (December 1985): 1117–34. The rendition in this paper is the immediate basis for the rendition here.

12 REED AND CANNON

Typically, parliamentary leaders can readily manipulate a parliamentary body. For example, prime ministers in cabinet governments like those of Britain or Germany are chairmen of the executive committee of the legislature and, as long as they hold office, are able thereby to dominate nearly everything that happens in the legislature. Even in less centralized governments like the United States, with its "separated powers" and three-house legislature, the chief officers of legislatures often are extremely influential. Speakers of the House are usually said to rate just below the president in political importance.

The basis for the strength of parliamentary leaders is their control over the order of business. In the structure of eighteenth-century parliaments, members, including leaders, were substantially equal. If any member brought up business—and any member could—then the body devoted itself to that business until the relevant stage of it was completed. Inside the parliament even the prime minister had very little more agenda-control than anyone else—his wider political authority came from the king's patronage, not from parliament.* By contrast, in most modern legislatures, the members have transferred their individual control over order to their leaders. It is this transferred authority that renders parliamentary leaders so politically strong.

But leaders are strong only so long as members wish it. If a united and disciplined majority stands behind a leader, thus

*The remnant of that eighteenth-century equality still exists in the United States Senate, where a member may speak as long as he is physically able, provided the Senate does not, by an extraordinary majority, impose closure. Even so, individual senators are not allowed to control the agenda directly.

itself *author*-izing his control, he then can manage business as he wishes and without apparent restraint. But let the majority lose its discipline, let a fraction of it break off so that a clear majority no longer exists, and the leader's authority vanishes. In parliamentary governments, all this is formalized: the prime minister holds office only until a majority votes against him.

That leaders' strength is by sufferance of members is vividly displayed in the history of the Speakership. It was, from the beginning, a notable office, but the concentration of control did not come about until 1890, when "Czar" Reed arrogated to himself the right to dominate. As it turned out, he probably went too far, so that in the "revolution of 1910," "Uncle Joe" Cannon, Reed's successor and a less skillful leader, was deprived of some, but not all, of the authority Reed had accumulated. The basic difference between the centralization of 1890 and the devolution of 1910 was a united, disciplined majority behind Reed, and a fragmented party no longer able to make a majority behind Cannon. Agenda-control is, as I have illustrated in several stories, a concentration of the opportunity for heresthetical manipulation. In effect, therefore, the united majority behind Reed authorized him to manipulate them, while the fragmented Republicans of 1910 would no longer tolerate manipulation.

It is an interesting fact that a majority of members came to want to be manipulated. The reason for this, I believe, was that rather suddenly in the 1880s many legislators were deeply frustrated. This was the era in which legislators, after nearly a century of governmental quietism (or "laissez-faire"), were just beginning to attempt to direct society by legislation. Since one man's direction is another man's tyranny, the opponents of the new legislative activism used the tools at hand to deter it. One major tool was the traditional equality of legislators, which became the basis, both in the U.S.A. and in Britain, for dilatory tactics. Expert delay made it difficult to get anything done. As a consequence, at any particular moment, more than half the members were frustrated because they could visualize a majority for some measure but they could not realize it.

Then Thomas B. Reed, a bold, creative parliamentarian, a man of wit, charm, and rhetorical brilliance, a Republican hero because of his verve and stagecraft, carried off one of the greatest heresthetical maneuvers in the long history of the Congress. In a few days at the end of January 1890, in a dramatic manipulation that captured the imagination of the whole country, he broke the legislative log-jam and thereby modernized the House. From then on, he was known as "Czar"—affectionately to Republicans, resentfully to Democrats.

During the 1880s, contrary to the usual interpretation, it was the Republicans who were legislative activists and Democrats who were dilatory. The parties were closely divided in almost every session, so it was easy for dilatory tactics to succeed. The main opponent of delay was Reed, the Republican specialist on parliamentary rules and, as minority leader from 1885 to 1889, the leading advocate of reform. He was elected Speaker late in 1889 and came to office with a promise of change, especially since the Harrison administration had accumulated a large and significant legislative program that ultimately resulted in, for example, the McKinley Tariff and the Sherman Anti-Trust Act. The party division was narrow, 168 Republicans to 161 Democrats, so the chance was small, given the expectation of delay, for enactment of the Republic program. Reed, therefore, planned to eliminate dilatory motions, to accelerate business in the Committee of the Whole, to empower the Speaker to handle many kinds of business automatically, and, most dramatically, to redefine a quorum.

For purposes of controlling the agenda, these reforms are significant in the order I have listed them. But from the point of view of public understanding, by far the most intriguing reform was the counting of a quorum. During the previous decade, the technique of the "disappearing quorum" had been perfected. A quorum is defined in the Constitution as a majority of the members. Since the framers were well aware of an earlier form of the disappearing quorum in which members physically absented themselves, they also provided for compulsion to attend to assure a quorum. The loophole exploited in the nineteenth century to create the new form of the disappearing quorum was to attend without voting. Traditionally, the existence of a quorum was discovered by taking the sum of the yeas and nays on a roll call. Hence, if a few persons were absent because of illness, travel, and so on, and if the margin between majority and minority was less than the number of absentees, the minority could deny a quorum simply by not voting. In the absence of a quorum business would then cease.

In January 1890, with a membership of 329, a quorum for the House was 165, and the Republicans had at most 168 in the caucus. Given illnesses and other factors, they usually could not by themselves guarantee a quorum. On 29 January, before the rules of the session were adopted, Reed and the Republicans moved consideration of a contested election case, which, when resolved, would of course ultimately result in another Republican member. The minority leader, Charles Crisp of Georgia, requested a decision on whether or not to consider the case. Had matters gone as usual for the era, the vote on the motion to consider would have revealed the absence of a quorum and the case would have been delayed until Republicans could get 165 of their 168 members on the floor.

But the new Speaker had a new plan. The motion to consider passed in a voice vote, Crisp called for the yeas and nays, and there were 161 yeas, 2 nays, and 165 not voting. The Congressional Record tells us what happened then:

> *The Speaker.* On this question, the yeas are 161, the nays 2.
> *Mr. Crisp.* No quorum.
> *The Speaker.* The chair directs the Clerk to record the following names of members present and refusing to vote: [Applause on the Republican side]
> *Mr. Crisp.* I appeal—[applause on the Democratic side]—I appeal from the decision of the Chair.
> *The Speaker.* Mr. Blanchard, Mr. Bland, Mr. Blount, Mr. Breckinridge, of Arkansas, Mr. Breckinridge, of Kentucky.
> *Mr. Breckinridge, of Kentucky.* I deny the power of the Speaker and denounce it as revolutionary. [Applause on the Democratic side of the House, which was renewed several times]
> *Mr. Bland.* Mr. Speaker—[Applause on the Democratic side]
> *The Speaker.* The House will be in order.

Mr. Bland. Mr. Speaker, I am responsible to my constituents for
the way in which I vote, and not to the Speaker of this House.
The Speaker. Mr. Brookshire, Mr. Bullock, Mr. Bynum, Mr. Car-
lisle, Mr. Chipman, Mr. Clements, Mr. Clunie, Mr. Compton.

Imperturbably and despite many interruptions, Reed continued to read from the list of 165 some names for the Clerk to
record as present. When he came to Mr. McCreary, this interchange took place:

Mr. McCreary. I deny your right, Mr. Speaker, to count me as
present, and I desire to read from the parliamentary law on
that subject.
The Speaker. The Chair is making a statement of the fact that the
gentleman from Kentucky is present. Does he deny it?
[Laughter and applause on the Republican side]
Mr. McCreary. The ruling of the Chair the other day contained the
following statement [cries of "Order!"]: . . .
The Speaker. The gentleman will be in order. [Laughter] The Chair
is proceeding in an orderly manner. [Renewed laughter and
applause on the Republican side] Mr. Montgomery, Mr.
Moore of Texas, Mr. Morgan.
Mr. Morgan. I beg leave to protest against this as unconstitutional
and revolutionary.
The Speaker (continuing). Mr. Outhwaite.
Mr. Outhwaite. [Cries of "Regular Order!"] I wish to state to the
Chair that I was not present in the House when my name was
called, and the Chair is therefore stating what is not true.
[Applause and cries of "Order!"] It is not for the Chair to say
whether I shall vote or not or whether I shall answer to my
name when it is called. [Laughter and applause]
The Speaker (continuing). Mr. Owens of Ohio, Mr. O'Ferrell.

And so forth, through about forty prominent Democrats. At
the end, and after much Democratic complaint, the Speaker
rationalized his decision:

There is a provision in the Constitution which declares that the
House may establish rules for compelling attendance of members.
If members can be present and refuse to exercise their function, to
wit, not to be counted as a quorum, that provision would seem to
be entirely nugatory. Inasmuch as the Constitution only provides

for their attendance, that attendance is enough. If more were needed, the Constitution would have provided more. . . . The Chair therefore rules that there is a quorum present within the meaning of the Constitution.

Of course, Crisp appealed the ruling and the debate continued for two more days. On both 30 and 31 January, Reed counted a quorum to approve the Journal. Finally, on 31 January, Reed counted a quorum to lay Crisp's appeal on the table and the election case was taken up. So Reed guided the House to business and a few days later it adopted revised rules that embodied all of Reed's reforms.

The critical element in Reed's management of this event seems to have been the care he took to see to it that he had every Republican on his side. His biographer tells us that he was prepared to resign if he failed, but of course he planned not to fail. Doubtless he had a good understanding of his caucus and sensed that his imperturbability in the face of three days of shouting, shoving, and angry speeches was fine theater. In effect, he turned the episode into a kind of sports match which the Repbulicans were sure to win as long as they supported him—and they did.*

The Democrats won the next election and went back to the earlier rules. But in 1894 Reed, as minority leader, forced the Speaker, now Crisp, to count a quorum just as Reed had done in 1890. Perhaps Reed was an even more adroit parliamentarian in the minority than in the majority. In any event, he was reelected Speaker in 1895; the House readopted the Reed rules of 1890 and kept them through three Speakers until 1910.

---

*The theatrical aspect was extremely important and appealed to the whole country. Later on in the session, once the quorum count was established, the only way to disappear was to leave physically. Reed plugged that loophole by ordering the sergeant at arms to lock the doors. On one such occasion, "Kicking Buck" Kilgore of Texas was so eager to get out that he broke down the door. Many storytellers have conflated these two events, the quorum call and Kilgore's exit, and it would have been even more theatrical if they had indeed occurred together. Unfortunately they did not, but still the drama of Reed's count remains one of the great events in the history of the House.

Reed succeeded, I believe, because he was always conscious of just whom he led. By contrast, Cannon was a mechanical man. He interpreted his nominal Republican majority as a real majority; and, when it turned out not to be real, he went down in degrading defeat. Both Reed and Cannon were economic conservatives, favoring hard money and high tariffs. Reed produced the McKinley tariff and Cannon the Payne-Aldrich tariff, and both these extreme measures led to Republican defeat in the next election. But Reed simply went down with his party and was not personally disgraced. He saw that he must keep his party together, so he used his influence to put through the Sherman Silver Purchase Act and the Sherman Anti-Trust Act, both of which were compromises, inside the Republican party, to cut the ground out from under more radical proposals from Democrats. Cannon, on the other hand, allowed for no compromises with Republican "progressives" or "insurgents" and used his power as much against them as against Democrats. He assumed that the progressives would not dare abandon the Republican name and were thus compelled to play by his rules. It did not occur to him, until too late, that they might continue to be Republicans but nevertheless revise the rules and disgrace him.

Reed dominated the House agenda by means of the Rules Committee, which he appointed and on which he sat. His reforms of dilatory tactics in effect removed impediments to his effective use of the committee to define the day-to-day agenda. Cannon inherited this arrangement, so an appropriate threat was to banish him from the Rules Committee. This was what his opponents attempted in March 1909 and carried through in March 1910.

On 15 March 1909 Cannon was reelected Speaker by a good margin, 204 to 166 for Champ Clark and a scattering of 12 for several insurgent Republicans. Still, Clark and the Democrats thought they could remove Cannon from the committee with the help of about 30 insurgents, who, as Republicans, would vote for Cannon for Speaker but vote against him on everything else. Indeed, the motion to adopt the old rules was rejected 189–193, with 29 insurgent Republicans voting with the

Democrats. Then Clark, as minority leader, moved for new rules that provided for the election by the House—not appointment by the Speaker. Cannon had, however, prepared for just this contingency. He had persuaded 22 Tammany and Southern Democrats to desert Clark for a substitute motion. The substitute left the Speaker and the Rules Committee intact, but provided for a modest elaboration of Calendar Wednesday to give members a chance to call up bills bottled up in committee. Cannon won 211 to 173. Even though 30 insurgent Republicans voted against the substitute, 22 Democrats supported it. Thus Cannon won by inducing in the Democratic party a split of about the same size as in the Republican party.

Had Cannon been required to deal only with the likes of Champ Clark, the Speakership might never have been reformed. But Cannon's really dangerous opponent was George Norris of Nebraska. Norris was the leader of the progressive Republicans in the House and a parliamentary tactician par excellence. Since Norris knew that not all insurgents were progressives, he carefully avoided an ideological attack, emphasizing always that the fight was not against party principles or party leadership, merely against the concentration of authority in the Speaker. Hence Norris attacked only the office, not the officer, to whom he was invariably polite and deferential, while blandly proposing to degrade the office.

Norris wrote out a motion to elect the Rules Committee and to prohibit the Speaker's membership on it. Then he attended every day, usually all day, waiting for an opportunity to surprise the Speaker by introducing it. Norris was confident that the Democrats and the insurgent Republicans would be a majority, especially since in a surprise move Cannon would be unable to subvert some Democrats as he had in 1909.

Norris's chance came on 16 March 1910, a Calendar Wednesday, when the Republican leadership called up an amendment to the Census Act for 1910, without properly dispensing (by two-thirds vote) with the call of committees. The amendment permitted the census to ask questions about "mother tongue" as well as nationality in order apparently to get a count of Czechs, Croats, and so on, whose numbers had been hidden under the category "Austrian." Haste was necessary on this otherwise trivial resolution because the 1910 enumeration was to begin in a few weeks. A point of order was raised against the resolution on the ground that it had improperly interrupted the call of committees. The Speaker ruled that matters relating to the census, which was provided for in the Constitution, raised a "constitutional question" which could thus displace business provided for simply under the rules of the House. Owing to the fact that many Republicans had left town for a spring vacation over St. Patrick's Day, the House rejected the Speaker's ruling by 112 to 163.

The defeat of the Speaker did not in any way reduce the need for haste on the census amendment so it was brought up again the next day, and the House was asked to take it up, again as a matter of "constitutional privilege." In the defense of this theory by a Republican regular, Norris saw his chance: "*Mr. Norris.* I want to ask the gentleman, on the constitutional proposition, if his theory is right, would it not follow that this [i.e., the joint resolution to amend the Census Act] would be in order, even though there was no report of a committee on the resolution? To make myself plain, if it is in order because the Constitution makes it in order, then the report of a Committee on the Census does not add anything to it. Would not that follow?" Falling into the trap, the regular responded: "*Mr. Olmstead.* It has been so held in election cases. . . . It was so ruled by Speaker Reed." Then, preparing for the situation he hoped soon to bring about: "*Mr. Norris:* Any Member could come in with a bill that had not even been printed [i.e., as Norris's would not be] and take up the time of the House on the ground that it was an amendment to the census law." Something about Norris's insistence induced wariness in Olmstead: "*Mr. Olmstead.* I think he would have to come in the regular way." Now Norris had what he wanted so he could agree pleasantly: "*Mr. Norris.* He would have to claim recognition, of course." And this is precisely what Norris planned.

The Speaker, having been repulsed the day before, did not

rule on whether or not the census amendment was in order but put the question directly to the House, which decided 201–72, to take up the census resolution, thereby inferentially endorsing the theory Norris had spun out.

Immediately after the House disposed of the census business, Norris was on his feet: "*Mr. Norris.* Mr. Speaker, I have a privileged resolution. . . . Mr. Speaker, I present a resolution made privileged by the Constitution." "*The Speaker.* If it is a resolution made privileged by the Constitution, the gentleman will present it. [Laughter]" Evidently the Speaker, wholly unaware of the trap, went through one of his famous contortions or mimicked Norris to bring on the laughter. But one can be sure the laughter died out as Norris handed his bombshell to the Clerk and as the Clerk read it. Norris's justification fit perfectly with his earlier interchange with Olmstead:

> The Constitution says we may make rules. We have just decided that when the Constitution gives us a right to do a thing, it is in order to bring in the proposition at any time. [Cries of "Oh, no!"] Let me finish. . . . This resolution is not a mandatory affair; it is something that the Constitution gives us the right to do, however. The gentlemen will have to admit that.
>
> The Constitution gives us the right to do this; consequently, when we bring in, under the constitutional provision, a resolution to do just what the Constitution gives us permission to do, I say, under the recent decision, it must be in order.

A point of order was, of course, made against Norris's motion and it was up to the Speaker to rule on it, something that should have been easy to for him to do because he had just had the precedents searched for the census resolution. But were he to rule either for or against Norris's motion, a vote would ultimately follow. And that vote Cannon was sure to lose with a hundred representatives, mainly Republicans, off on vacation. So Cannon delayed, hoping to get Republicans back. The insurgents and Democrats, on the other hand, tried to force the Speaker to rule by keeping the House in continuous session, all the rest of Thursday on to 2:00 in the afternoon on Friday. At 2:00 there was a recess until 4:00 P.M., during which it was agreed that the Speaker would rule on Saturday at noon. The bad position of the regular Republicans was revealed in four motions to adjourn on Thursday night and Friday morning. These motions failed by 142–147, 137–146, 141–142, and 134–141. The regular leadership devoted most of Thursday and Friday to telephoning absentees, and the all-night session must have been pretty hard on Cannon, who was seventy years old. Indeed, I suspect that the continuous session had something to do with his agreement to rule on Saturday.

Cannon, of course, ruled against Norris's resolution, and then followed, in quick succession:

a. Norris's appeal to the floor on the Speaker's ruling;
b. a vote on a motion to adjourn (failed, on a voice vote);
c. a vote to lay Norris's resolution on the table (failed, 164–182, with 6 present and 37 absent);
d. a vote on the previous question (i.e., for an immediate vote) on Norris's appeal (passed, 183–160, with 7 present and 39 absent);
e. a vote on sustaining the Speaker's ruling (failed, 162–182, with 7 present and 37 absent);
f. a brief debate on Norris's resolution and his substitute (which contained a method of electing the Rules Committee more acceptable to Democrats than was his original method);
g. a vote on the previous question on the substitute (passed, 180–159, with 7 present and 42 absent);
h. a vote on the substitute itself (passed, 193–153, with 5 present and 38 absent) and, finally;
i. a vote on Norris's perfected resolution (passed, 191–156, with 5 present, and 37 absent.

Thus, in just a few hours, the Speaker was sharply rebuked by having the essential character of his office changed.

Norris then moved to adjourn so that the Speaker's shame could not be concealed. But the Speaker asked for a chance to make a statement and Norris, ever polite, acquiesced. The Speaker tried to retrieve his position by demanding a vote on himself personally. A Democrat then appropriately moved to vacate the office. Norris tried to prevent the motion by reviving his motion to adjourn. But now both regular Republicans and Democrats wanted a roll call and Norris could not even get the yeas and nays on his rejected motion to adjourn. (The Constitution provides for the yeas and nays if one-fifth requests it, but Norris had only 14 supporters.) The regulars wanted a vote because they believed the insurgents would support Cannon and thus take the sting out of the motion just passed. The Democrats wanted a vote because they believed the insurgents would support the motion to vacate the office.

The regulars were right. The House rejected the motion to vacate, 155–192, with 8 present and 33 absent. So Cannon retrieved something, but not very much. In the fall elections, the Democrats won and Republicans did not regain the House until 1918, by which time the House had fully accepted the new situation of a Rules Committee completely independent of the Speaker. So the Rules Committee was not changed again until 1974—but that is another story.

Cannon had, throughout most of his career, indeed even through most of his Speakership, been a party man, seeking always to reconcile differences, jocularly building rapport with every Republican. But in 1908 he undertook to stamp out progressivism, and he used the full advantage of his office to put through the Payne-Aldrich tariff and several other highly conservative measures. He had reason to suppose he could succeed because there were a few more Republican regulars than the sum of Democrats and insurgent Republicans. But he could not stop spring vacations and he could not stop George Norris. So he lost his majority and a good part of the authority that Reed had so carefully accumulated.

All this is a way of saying that the heresthetical resources of parliamentary leaders are entirely dependent on a supportive majority. Reed knew this but Cannon forgot it.

Sources: The quotations in this chapter are from the *Congressional Record,* 51st Cong., 1st sess., 29 January 1890, pp. 949–

50, and 61st Cong., 2nd sess., 17 March 1910, pp. 3285 and 3291–92.

A good biography of Reed is William A. Robinson, *Thomas B. Reed: Parliamentarian* (New York: Dodd, Mead and Co., 1930), and good accounts of the revolution of 1910 are Blair Bolles, *Tyrant from Illinois: Uncle Joe Cannon's Experiment with Personal Power* (New York: W. W. Norton, 1951), and William Rea Gwinn, *Uncle Joe Cannon: Archfoe of Insurgency: A History of the Rise and Fall of Cannonism* (Baltimore: Bookman Associates, 1957).

CONCLUSION

Most people seem to believe that voting is pretty simple. People cast ballots; someone adds them up; and, presto, there is a straightforward decision. But voting is not at all simple. All these stories are about voting, and in every one of them voting does not turn out as expected. Some people might, however, say: "But these are all special cases that you chose because they were pathological. Most of the time voting really is simple." I confess that I did choose the stories for their interest, but I deny that they are abnormal in any other way. They depict politics as it usually is, with politicians continually poking and pushing the world to get the results they want.

The reason they do this is they believe (and rightly so) that they can change outcomes by their efforts. It is often the case that voting need not have turned out the way it did. This fact is easy to overlook because it is hard to compare what did happen with what might have happened. But sometimes comparison is possible, as in the story about the flying club and the Plott-Levine experiment. In that experiment, at least three sets of people with the same structure of preference produced different outcomes from voting because some herestheticians (in this case Plott and Levine) had set up the agendas differently. What happened in the laboratory can happen in the world of nature. So politicians are constantly trying to manipulate agendas.

The reason why agendas are manipulable and indeed why, in general, all institutions are manipulable is that for no such institution can it be guaranteed in all cases that the social choice will be independent of the method by which it was chosen. (This is indeed one way of stating Arrow's theorem, which is the fundamental theorem of social choice theory.) And if the choice depends in part on the way it was chosen, then politicians can reasonably expect to change the outcome if they can change the way that questions are posed, or the considerations that influence participants' judgment, or the way votes are counted, or which votes are counted, and so on.

What comes out of the machine for aggregation is popularly said to be the "will of the people." Sometimes it may be, though we never know for sure and we never know when. Mostly, however, it is, as social choice theory tells us, some unanticipated combination of the wills of participants and of the way the relevant politicians have set the machine to implement their own wills. Such an outcome is hardly the will of the people; it is just some choice that came out of the machine. Most politicians would prefer, however, that it be their own choice rather than the choice of some other politician. The stories in this book are simply examples of their efforts to see that it is their own preferred choice that is chosen.

One way to visualize this situation is in a simple and rather specialized form of the social choice model. This model reveals why, when voters continue to have the same tastes, different alternatives can be chosen with different methods of voting. From that fact nearly everything else follows.

I

In this model there are:

1. People, who are characterized by a set of values and tastes, by the ability to order these tastes, and by the ability to take appropriate action in light of the ordering;
2. Alternatives, which are conceivable choices for society and which are defined as possible combinations of locations on one or more dimensions in a geometric model of the political world;
3. The dimensions themselves, which are standards of measurement for relevant variable properties of alternatives and tastes, and;
4. Some methods of choosing, here majority rule.

Both alternatives and individual choices (i.e., individual preferences among conceivable alternatives) are located in the space defined by one or more dimensions. In figure 1, there are two dimensions, x and y, which, in the case of an impending decision on, say, a school budget, might be measures of the desired range of teachers' salaries and of the desired student-teacher ratio. A particular point, say (x_2, y_2), is a combination of person two's judgment in favor of a relatively small amount on the x axis and a relatively large amount on the y axis. Point (x_1, y_1) is person one's ideal point (or, uniquely best combination) with respect to the two dimensions—that is, the point at which he would be most pleased. Similarly, (x_2, y_2) and (x_3, y_3) are ideal points for persons two and three.

For convenience of exposition here, I assume that, between any pair of alternative points, say j and k, a person prefers the alternative closest to his ideal. Thus, person one prefers j to k because j is closer to (x_1, y_1) than is k, while person three prefers k to j for a similar reason. Such a regularity of preferences is not necessary in a more complicated model, but here I assume it to simplify the exposition geometrically.

If only one dimension, say x, were the basis for judgment,

FIGURE 1

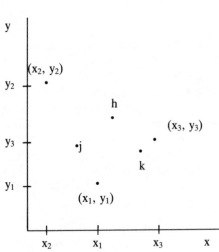

all the ideal points would lie on the horizontal axis itself, as shown in figure 1 with the labels x_1, x_2, and x_3. In one dimension it turns out that there is an obvious winner by majority rule, namely, point x_1, in the middle. If x_1 were put against any point to its left, say x_2, then x_1 would win by majority rule because persons one and three would choose x_1 inasmuch as x_1 is closer to their ideals than is x_2. Similarly, if x_1 were put against any point to its right, say x_3, then persons one and two would prefer x_1 to x_3. Thus x_1 can beat any other conceivable alternative on the x dimension. And x_1 is a strong equilibrium of tastes in the sense that participants choose it over all others, and, having chosen it, stick with it, and, if displaced from it, revert to it when possible. This point, x_1, the median on the dimension, is in balance because the persons not at the median are equally balanced (equilibrated, indeed) on each side of the median.

One can think of an equilibrium as something that, within the model, is certain to happen because it is the effect of a cause. A necessary and sufficient condition (that is, a cause) for some x_1 to be an equilibrium in one dimension (given majority rule and an odd number of voters) is that, when voters always strictly prefer points closer to their ideal to points further away, x_1 is the ideal point of the median voter. The intellectual advantage of the existence of an equilibrium is that it is a predictable and certain consequence of individual tastes and values. To the extent that the world is like the model and contains no institutional distortions, the world also has a predictable and certain outcome.

This neat equilibrium in one dimension does not carry over to two dimensions. In figure 1, if only the y dimension is considered, y_3 is the median. But the combination of x_1 and y_3, representing, as it does, two different persons, is not a possible median, though it is a possible outcome. Hence the equilibrium based on a median person (usually) disappears in two dimensions, unless the participants are arranged so that the same person is the median on both dimensions and so that pairs of non-median persons lie on a line through the median and on opposite sides of it.

Assuming that difficult condition is not met, there is no equilibrium. Instead, if we suppose that persons one and two agree on adopting j, then persons two and three would prefer to replace j with h, persons one and three would prefer to replace h with k, and finally, to complete the cycle, person one and two would prefer to replace k with j. The three voters might go around this cycle indefinitely, which is exactly what is meant by disequilibrium or a lack of balance.

As the geometry makes vividly clear, it is easy to visualize equilibrium in one dimension, but the equilibrium is rare and unlikely in two dimensions even with as few as three voters. In the absence of equilibrium, nothing about the distribution of ideal points and nothing about the institution of majority voting forces the social choice to a unique and predictable outcome. Consequently, one expects the voters to move around from j to h, from h to k, and so on, until someone stops the process by active intervention. This is why in this abstract model the complications of two dimensions (or more) guarantee that many outcomes are possible. Which one occurs depends, of course, on how clever and skillful people stop the process to their advantage.

II

How well does this simple model capture the essential features of the real world? Suppose a real society uses pure majority rule as, for example, in the New England town meeting. Then this model is rather obviously a simplified version of society. Suppose, at the other extreme, social institutions provide for a dictator, for example, a judge appointed for life. Then there will be much more observable stability than in the town meeting, but it is of a random kind, because the outcomes for the whole society do not depend on the opinions of people in the society but rather on the accident of who happens to be the judge. Cycles of opinion may well exist in the whole society, of course, and would appear if there were some institutional arrangement to discover them. But since the judge decides, the cycles are hidden beneath the individual consistency of the judge. One would not wish to describe such a system as being in equilibrium, however, because the characteristic dissatisfaction of disequilibrium remains. By definition of a cycle, some majority is opposed to each alternative. If a cycle exists and a judge chooses some alternative in it, then the resentment in society is just as real and divisive as when a representative legislature, perhaps manipulated by an agenda, chooses an unpopular alternative. In either case, there is some majority that knows it might have won, had the institutions permitted it.

Suppose institutions lie somewhere between the extremes of pure democracy and dictatorship as, for example, in a system requiring extraordinary majorities to change the status quo, a system we approximate in the United States by having a three-house legislature (house of representatives, senate, and, conditionally, the president). Since the status quo is greatly advantaged in all decisions, stability is commonly observed; but, again, it is a random stability based on the pre-existing status quo and the particular set of representatives inherited from the last election. There will be many cycles of opinion in society and many, but fewer, cycles of opinion in the legislature. But there will also be equilibrium imposed simply by the fact that it is difficult to get an extraordinary majority together. In that sense, institutions and the dead hand of the past along with, occasionally, the values of people in society influence outcomes. And any particular outcome is some unpredictable combination of influence from the values of the past and values of the present.

I conclude, therefore, that the model does capture what is important for understanding heresthetic—namely, the fact of disequilibrium in the political world.

III

The events described in this book can be distributed into three categories: agenda control, strategic voting, and manipulations of dimensions. Each kind of manipulation can be explained in terms of the model.

1. Agenda control. This category contains the stories about:
   Plott and Levine (chapter 3);

Pliny (chapter 7);
Reed (chap. 12);
Norris (chap. 12).

In the Plott-Levine experiment, which is the purest instance of agenda control, there was an equilibrium of preferences. In this case, the equilibrium choice is a so-called Condorcet winner, which is that alternative which, if it exists, can beat every other alternative in a head-to-head vote. Alternative A was the Condorcet winner and, had a round robin been conducted, it certainly would have won. There was only one dimension on which to evaluate the alternatives, namely, the different amounts of money payoffs. So the alternatives could be arranged on that dimension in just the way alternatives are arranged on the horizontal axis of figure 1, with A as the ideal point of the median voter. The experimenters' problem was to make B, C, and D winners in the face of the equilibrium for A. Similarly, Pliny faced a Condorcet winner—that is, banishment—probably in one dimension (the amount of punishment from zero to death), while he wanted acquittal to win.

In both cases the problem of agenda control is to defeat what is, on paper, the certain winner. The device each used was to group the alternatives for voting in such a way that the Condorcet winner was eliminated. Plott and Levine did this by pitting the set containing A against another set that was, on balance, more attractive. Hence A was eliminated at the first stage of the process and some alternative inferior to A in a pairwise vote could still emerge as a winner in the last stage of the process. Similarly, Pliny's ternary procedure permitted the plurality winner, acquittal, even though banishment could beat it in a pairwise vote.

In chapter 12 there are two instances of agenda control. Normally in legislative roll calls there are just two alternatives, yes and no, and one must win. But Reed's opponents expected to beat him by producing a third alternative, abstain, which under the quorum rules had an advantage and was indeed an institutional equilibrium. Reed refused to allow this third alternative to appear, so his preferred alternative won in a pairwise vote. Conversely, Norris expected that his alternative for the election of the Rules Committee—which he rightly believed to be the equilibrium outcome—would be ruled out of order. So he laid his trap and waited several months until he found a situation in which something similar was ruled to be in order. Then he placed his motion on the floor before Cannon could stop him and thereby, though a back-bencher, momentarily seized control of the agenda.

2. Strategic voting. This category contains the stories about:
  Pliny (chap. 7);
  Massachusetts and South Carolina delegates (chap. 8);
  Chichester (chap. 9);
  The Anti-School Aid Republicans (chap. 11);
  Chrystal's final vote—perhaps (chap. 5);
  Morris et al., on McClurg's motion (chap. 4).

Strategic voting is, in a sense, the flip side of agenda control. For the most part, the formal leadership of the decision-making body controls the agenda (except in special cases like that of Norris). But individual members, whether leaders or not, control their own votes. Given an agenda, they can sometimes win by appropriate use of their vote resource. This is an especially vivid possibility in the case of Pliny's opponent, who could reverse an act of agenda control by strategic voting. Pliny had made acquittal a certain winner, so he believed, as long as his opponents voted myopically for their most preferred alternative. But some of his opponents voted strategically for their second choice. Thus they both beat Pliny and won something for themselves.

Most of the other cases of strategic voting similarly involve the defeat of an apparently certain winner—indeed, an equilibrium outcome—by voting in such a way as to upset the equilibrium. This is what vote-traders, like the Massachusetts and South Carolina delegates, do, thereby passing two motions that might otherwise be expected to lose. This is what Chrystal did with his vote switch, though by the time he acted his preference had come to conform with his intended action. This is what Chichester did by not voting. His myopic preference, which the lieutenant-governor expected to exploit, was to vote no but by abstaining strategically he obtained his best outcome.

In this book the only instance of strategic voting that failed to upset an equilibrium was the voting by Morris, Madison, et al. on McClurg's motion. They voted against what Madison tells us was their true taste in order to show that election of the executive by the legislature necessarily involved intrigue. Thus they were using the tactic of strategic voting to introduce a new dimension, which in turn was intended to upset an equilibrium. So perhaps this last instance really belongs in my third category, manipulation of dimensions.

3. Manipulation of dimensions. This category contains the stories about:
   Lincoln (chap. 1);
   DePew (chap. 2);
   Chrystal (chap. 5);
   City Manager (chap. 6);
   Magnuson (chap. 10); and, in part,
   Morris (chap. 4)

Often it is difficult to control the agenda or to vote strategically, especially if the equilibrium winner has a substantial majority. But the number of dimensions can always be used to upset an equilibrium, provided the heresthetician is clever enough to find the correct dimension to use. This, no doubt, is why manipulation of dimensions is just about the most frequently attempted heresthetical device, one that politicians engage in a very large amount of the time.

It is easy to see why it works. Suppose there is an equilibrium in one dimension, as on the horizontal axis of figure 1. (There need not be, of course, for there may be a cycle of opinion; but very often equilibrium does exist in one dimension and the heresthetical problem is to break it up in an advantageous way.) Suppose, then, a second dimension is introduced, like the vertical axis of figure 1. Person one, the median voter on x, moves only a short distance on y, while persons two and three move further. The median voter on y is person three. Now the equilibrium is lost. On a vote that puts, say x_1, the initial status quo, on the horizontal axis, against, say h, h will win because persons two and three will prefer h to x_1. But h can lose to j, and so forth. Just what will win is unclear, but certainly x_1 will be eliminated and person two will think himself wise to have introduced the new dimension.

Most of the great shifts in political life result from introducing a new dimension. Thus, the use of the issue of slavery to break up the equilibrium in which Jeffersonians and Jacksonians were the median voters on the economic dimension was the main political maneuver of the nineteenth century. The process took forty years, and Lincoln's heresthetical contribution was built on the heresthetic of Rufus King and John Quincy Adams.

But the manipulation of dimensions also is effective on smaller scales. DePew could (at least for a while) break up the putative majority for direct election by introducing the dimension of a force bill. Magnuson could break up the majority for bringing back nerve gas by introducing the dimension of the dignity of the Senate. Morris could break up the majority for election of the executive by the legislature by bringing up the advantage that small states might expect from electors. Conversely, the city manager of chapter 6 could prevent what might well have been a Republican majority by making it impossible to bring up the dimension of fairness (i.e., of the gerrymander). And in a somewhat different vein, Chrystal forced Jago and Crawford to vote for each other by raising the specter of the Visitor.

So, in both the large and the small, the manipulation of dimensions is a major part of heresthetics. This manipulation works even though those who are manipulated know they are being manipulated because, once a salient dimension is revealed, its salience exists regardless of one's attitude toward it. It may be that this is why the manipulation of dimensions is the preferred heresthetical maneuver; once performed it does its work without further exertion by the heresthetician.

Suggestions for Further Reading
The only elementary, nonmathematical introductory book on social choice theory is William H. Riker, *Liberalism against*

Populism: A Confrontation between the Theory of Democracy and the Theory of Social Choice (San Francisco: W. H. Freeman Co., 1982). Just a step up mathematically are: Charles Plott, "Axiomatic Social Choice Theory," *American Journal of Political Science* 20 (August 1976): 511–96; and Amartya K. Sen, *Collective Choice and Social Welfare* (San Francisco: Holden-Day, 1970). The current technical literature, which is spread around in many journals, can perhaps best be approached through the quarterly journal *Social Choice and Welfare,* published by Springer International, Berlin.